REDEEMING
MARRIAGE

"It is a moving, at times eloquent reflection on the most basic relationship we have. . . . I appreciate the hopefulness that permeates the book and welcome your clear affirmation that our hope is grounded in our faith.

"All in all, a fine celebration of partnership, the partnership of men and women, and of humans and good."

JAMES CARROLL

"He has written with genuine feeling out of his deep convictions. . . . In an age that tends to take marriage lightly and cynically, his high view of it reminds us of what, at its richest, it can become."

FREDERICK BUECHNER

"A wonderfully wise and heartwarming book, making a spirited defense of marriage. . . . The splendid format subjects the marriage service to a line-by-line theological analysis and illustrates it with vivid and apt vignettes. The book is timely, authoritative, and graceful."

CHARLES PRICE
Virginia Theological Seminary

"A book that will provide for others, as it did for me, a marvelous medium for getting inside one's own marriage relationship. I never got the feeling of 'ought' from this book, but rather a feeling of how great our possibilities in the relationship might be. . . . It will be very useful for anyone helping couples prepare for marriage or guiding a couple in reflection when things are not going so well."

PHILIP SMITH
Bishop of New Hampshire

D1444059

Redeeming Marriage

Edward S. Gleason

COWLEY PUBLICATIONS
Cambridge ✦ *Boston*
Massachusetts

Published in the United States of America by Cowley
Publications, a division of the Society of St. John the Evangelist.
No portion of this book may be reproduced, stored in or
introduced into a retrieval system, or transmitted, in any form or
by any means—including photocopying—without the prior
written permission of Cowley Publications, except in the case of
brief quotations embodied in critical articles and reviews.

Library of Congress Cataloging in Publication Data:
Gleason, Edward S., 1933–
Redeeming marriage / Edward S. Gleason
    p.   cm.
ISBN: 0-936384-55-7 (pbk.)
1. Marriage—Religious aspects—Episcopal Church. 2. Episcopal
Church—Doctrines.   3. Anglican Communion—Doctrines. 4.
Episcopal Church. Celebration and blessing of a marriage. 5.
Gleason, Edward S., 1933– .   I. Title.
BX5949.M3G54 1988
265′.5—dc 19   87-29960

Sixth printing

This book is printed on recycled, acid-free paper and was
produced in the United States of America.

Cowley Publications
28 Temple Place
Boston, Massachusetts 02111

for

A.V.G.

through whose grace all things remain

TABLE OF CONTENTS

ACKNOWLEDGMENTS

This book was written during a six month sabbatical that Anne and I enjoyed in Santa Fe, New Mexico. These were days like no others we have known. The atmosphere, the warmth, the spirituality of Santa Fe are without flaw; creativity abounds in many forms, inviting thoughtful reflection. No one more embodied Santa Fe for us than Peggy Pond Church, whom we met in the story of her life in New Mexico, detailed in her writings, and described for us first at her Memorial Service. Would that we could have known her, but her story and that of her marriage are very alive in the fifteen sonnets, *The Ripened Fields*, herein frequently and gratefully quoted.

Cynthia Shattuck's insight, inspiration, and knowledge brought this book into reality; she is a unique professional, whose talent is her ministry.

Grateful thanks to Theodore McConnell, who early encouraged my writing, and to Frederick Buechner, James Carroll, Charles Price and Philip Smith, each of whom graciously and thoughtfully read and commented on these pages.

Before this book was conceived, while it was being written, and after its completion, more and more it became clear that everything I know and value results from the marriage it has been my good fortune to experience. One person made that marriage possible—Anne.

- E.S.G.

REDEEMING
MARRIAGE

PROLOGUE

He had opened the curtains. Back in bed, he lay, silent, staring across her at the reddening of the eastern sky. He hugged her tighter.

Once the morning started, the new day would not stop. He wished it would. It was just one more day, one day closer to the end. Who ever said, "Hold back the dawn!"? He knew why. The morning did not bring joy; the morning brought another day.

They'd often talked together about the night terrors. Everyone had them, she had said; she was right. Things get bent out of proper shape in the dark. Bearings are lost, perception distorted. What vision there is, is poor, misshapen, scary. This was what the Psalmist meant when he sang that weeping may spend the night. But this particular night, many nights in fact, had been different. Night had become the time to feel close, in touch, arms and legs wrapped around the other, the only one. The one who knows me and who I am and what I feel and even who I would be. At night we are one flesh. There is hope, and there is love, and there is affirmation.

The sky grows red. It will soon be day. Day brings fear and separation, the trivial round and common task which, despite the familiar words of the hymn, do not furnish all we ought to ask. Day means assuming a role, playing a part. Here and now, it is still night. He is at home and at peace and in love, connected in mind, body, and spirit to the one other person who knows him through and through and loves him still.

One more day meant one day closer to the end of all that made it possible to live another day. Some might say this meant he was afraid to die. Perhaps. He did not think so. Who could be afraid of death, if it is just one long night? That did not frighten him. Death was only frightening as the everlasting end of that very night which gave him new life, every night, night after night.

While there was still night, there was union. Separation came in the morning, as he rose to act out the business of being alive. At night, there was no acting. At night, it was all real. He hugged her tighter and allowed his mind to wander in reverie, devotion, awe. Robert Louis Stevenson had written of a magic time at dusk. Well and good. The time just at dawn had a different kind of magic.

He remembered the haunting words, "Dawn is a time when the world has other owners." Dawn was the time when they belonged, and that ownership was a gift, a gift from the one who lay breathing, rising and falling, so slowly, so steadily, within his arms. Without her there would be no dawn, for there would be no reason to rise, to greet the day, even to have a day. Why did the day mean so very often that they must be parted? Parting was not sweet sorrow. Parting was pain.

The sky grew ever brighter. He withdrew one arm from around her body and slipped it up and under her long white nightgown and began to rub her back. At first, soft, round, sweeping motions. Then, firm, rhythmical massage, hard, purposeful, up and down, up and down her backbone, and up through the opening at the neck, through her hair, and then down. She stirred, reached around, mumbled, began to caress his thigh, and he came alive, stiff and hard. They began to talk, wild, rambling bursts and exclamations. The early hours were often full of love talk, sometimes serious, often crazy, blending the night dreams of each other with the morning embrace, infused and surrounded by the increasing daylight.

Suddenly, slowly, with no warning, she rolled over and lay flat. Hands stretched up, the nightgown came off, and then, without pause, in one continuous motion, she pulled him over on top of her. Deliciously, forcefully, passionately, they made love.   Motion, skin, warmth, contact, minutes, closeness, intimacy born of years of living, sharing, union, memories, all blending together in rhythm, a diffusion of warmth, release and ultimate relaxation. Disappointment. It is over. But assurance and hope that throughout this particular day, there will be no separation, none at all. Only the things which remain.

SOMETHING COMPLETE AND GREAT

The purpose of life is to spend it for something that outlives us.

William James

Once upon a time there was a little boy. At first he was not just any little boy; he was unusual. People told him he was cute, and when it came time to go to school, he was smarter than most others. He received prizes and praise; the world smiled.

But then he grew up. He had some friends, not many. More and more he was alone. One had to earn friendship, even love. People were more affectionate and offered approval when you proved you deserved it, and approval was important.

Then he went to a big, important school, and suddenly, sadly, the boy was very much alone and certain that no one loved him. For at that big, important school, there were big, important people, and you were only loved if your were big and important too, and the boy was really very little and lonely and scared, and the school told him that he was just ordinary and not worth being loved.

Summer came, and back at the lake he saw the girl he had met for the first time right before he went away to school. She was not just any girl. She weighed a hundred and ten pounds and had a turned-up nose, and she liked to listen and talk, and he liked to talk and listen. Sometimes at night, in the woods, all alone together, they would talk to each other about everything —happy times, sad times, questions, loneliness. They were not in love; they really didn't know what they were, only that they were little and lonely and scared.

But when it was autumn, they both returned to school. Sometimes they wrote, and then summer came again. Suddenly, wonderfully, they were never quite sure how or why, they were best friends, and then they were lovers, and that was an amazing thing. Not because there is no love in the world, but because most of it is conditional. This was different. It wasn't earned. It was given, given from one person to the other, even though each knew really all there was to know about the other and it wasn't all good. Yet they discovered as a great gift, on a beautiful starry night, alone in the middle of the lake, that they were in love. That was the best discovery of all their lives.

Years after, late at night, they would lie in bed together and wonder how they could possibly be so lucky. Their story was a miracle. Gradually, sometimes painfully, they came to realize something more—that this miracle story was like another, well-known story about a man who offered the same kind of unconditional love to the same kind of ordinary people. He loved them so much that he was willing to die for them, and this made all the difference, for then no one had to be little and lonely and scared.

And when the boy and girl grew up, finally, sometime between the ages of thirty and forty, they suddenly realized that everything they knew, everything they valued, everything they learned, everything that was important all started with that special moment when they knew they were no longer ordinary, but loved.

"And what are you going to be when you grow up?"

Without a moment of hesitation the child answers, "Married."

"You have answered well. Do not be anxious about your life, what you shall eat or what you shall drink, or even what you shall do."

This is a book about being married. It is *not* a book about what we do but who we are, and who we become, one with the other. Therefore this is really a book for everyone, for each of us lives in some relationship to marriage—the marriage which, quite literally, gave us life, or the marriage in which we chose to live, and even the marriage in which we chose not to live. But this is not a book for unthinking people. Rather it is a book for those who wish to reflect in a Christian context about being married. They may be people preparing to become married for the first time, or people who have ended a less than sucessful marriage and prepare now to enter a new and different marriage. Or they may be those who help others to think about marriage.

The book may be read quickly, at a sitting, or more slowly, as a meditation, to provide certain shocks of recognition, moments when we see ourselves, just as we are, but in new ways, too. Despite the narcissism of our adolescence, from which we never fully depart, our experience in marriage, no matter how personal or how special, is never unique. In marriage we are united not only to one single other human being but also to a great body of persons, most of whom we do not know, who also live in marriages.

If there is a religious moment, a religious experience, in our lifetime, it is found in marriage. No matter what our heritage or background, no matter what our hopes or dreams, no matter what our profession or livelihood, in marriage we face ourself and one other and a clear choice. In such a time as this God is present. The choice is always ours, but God is within the choice; this is a book of theological perspective.

That perspective is set in the context of The Celebration and Blessing of a Marriage from The Book of Common Prayer of the Episcopal Church. This marriage liturgy is a rich source, refined and emended through the wisdom and experience of several generations, to enable us to live in the power of Christian marriage. That is an opportunity like no other we shall ever know —to create, to meet, to be—with one other and in the presence of a great cloud of witnesses. This book asks you to consider anew this opportunity. Is it realistic? As it is understood in the marriage liturgy, Christian marriage is not realistic at all, not a description of how things are, but rather a description of what might be, the reality of Christ that is both present and also still always on the verge of becoming, more and more.

People who marry face two decisions more important than any others: the choice of spouse and the choice of vocation. The world and all that is in it constantly reminds us that we are what we do. Not so. We become what we are through being loved by one other person, different from anyone else—the person whom we chose and by whom we are chosen to marry.

Yet the choice of a spouse is a decision for which we have little preparation. How do we undertake this choice, always a great and undeserved gift? These reflections on marriage are one attempt. They are shaped by the conviction that marriage is an essential religious choice and the understanding that religion lives in our choices, for religion is what we take seriously with no reservations.

The Christian religion is rooted in Christ's love, whose continuing revelation comes to us through the presence and person of others. Nowhere is this more clear than in marriage, because marriage is the crucial and powerful revelation of the presence and person of Jesus Christ. To be married means to be Christ one to another, the Christ who loved us when we did not deserve it. His love is ours and ours alone in the love of our own beloved. It is the power and presence of the love of Christ, who loved with all of his life, even to death, his own bride, the Church. This Christ dwells in our very midst in marriage.

For those whose wedding follows the service in the Book of Common Prayer, that liturgy provides a common understanding of marriage. The words are familiar. We may have heard them so many times in this and earlier versions that we know them by heart. Yet seldom, especially at the moment of the wedding itself, do we take the time to reflect upon them. The words of the liturgy are few in number, chosen with care, combined to form a vivid tapestry. It is a tapestry that illustrates what marriage is when it takes place in the name and presence and power of Our Lord Jesus Christ.

The love of Christ expressed in marriage is not based upon any service, function or act. It is not based on merit, or on good behavior, or on complete and total fulfillment of any code or agreement. It is based only on love, freely offered, freely received, undeserved. To be married means to be redeemed. To be married is to be loved only for who we are, not who we might wish to be or who we might seem to be. To be married means more than living together, more than going on vacations together, more than providing a series of goods and services for each other. To be married means to be Christ one to another.

Willa Cather wrote, "That is happiness, to be dissolved into something complete and great."

DEARLY BELOVED

THE EXHORTATION

Dearly Beloved: We have come together in the presence of God

The words shout. Familiar from book titles, poems, movies, soap operas, they announce and introduce. Reminiscent, but more powerful than "Hey, everyone, I'm home!" or "Wait until you hear what I have to say!", there is a tone of gravity. The stage is set for serious conversation, not unlike a long awaited heart-to-heart between lover and beloved, parent and child.

The words are concise, their business quite clear. Marriage has to do with God—the center of all that is, was, and will be.

to witness and bless the joining together of this man and this woman in Holy Matrimony.

This is not a private matter. It is a public event. Marriage is the business of two individuals, but it is undertaken within a greater company of witnesses, supporters, and friends. Apart from such witnesses, a marriage does not take place.

*   *   *

. . . The very young couple, obviously nervous and scared, appeared at the minister's door as the sun was setting one hot and humid July evening. They came from across the state line, to a place where there were no family or acquaintances, to ask him to officiate at their marriage—in complete privacy. "Please, could we do it all right now, quickly and quietly?"

"But surely your parents, your family and friends will want to be present? This is a time for the creation of memories and great celebration."

"No. You don't understand. This is our business and ours alone. No one need know, not right away, not until after the baby is born." And then it was all clear.

The marriage was not to be celebrated that night, nor even the next morning. It was celebrated some weeks later in the presence of God and the face of a large and joyful company of family and friends, who stood together to witness and support. Otherwise it just could not have happened. The day was not dark, and they were not scared, though still young and full of hope and promise.

The bond and covenant of marriage was established by God in creation,

Marriage is not just a piece of paper, nor a matter of social custom and convenience. Marriage is a part of the original and natural order of things, established by God as the way a man and a woman are to live together in God's world. Despite the clouds of romance which so often surround it, the marriage liturgy is a strong document full of "hard" statements, clear but perhaps difficult conditions, not easily nor always fulfilled. The liturgy is not meant to be intimidating, but it is certainly straightforward, stating realities that we cannot avoid save at the peril of our marriage. These realities begin with the statement that "the bond and covenant of marriage was established by God in creation." This is an understanding of the natural order, the way things are to be, now and henceforward. Nothing is to alter this.

*   *   *

. . . Seven couples, all married, had gathered for a relaxed evening. They sat around lazily, laughing and joking. Small groups formed and then dissolved. Too newly married, most of them, to have thought—yet—of extramarital adventure, nevertheless, it was no accident when these two sat side by side. There had been more than one look exchanged between them. She found him desirable. Caught within a marriage which was never to satisfy her, sexually or spiritually, she was different from the others, already jaded, almost desperate. Younger, happier, more naive, he admitted only to himself that he found her seductive. It was a warm September night, the mood jovial, the breeze caressing. She was often at his side, and then remained. Her leg, bare, smooth, tan, inviting, rubbed against his. He adjusted his position; the pressure returned, more forceful, insistent, inviting. The invitation, known only to the two of them, apparently unimportant, was in fact a crossroads whose implications were lifelong. Then, with just as little warning, in the very next moment, there was the opportunity to move away from her. He took it.

and our Lord Jesus Christ adorned this manner of life by his presence and first miracle at a wedding in Cana of Galilee.

This reference to the Gospel of John points to Jesus' choice of a wedding as the first significant event of his public life. The changing of water into wine signified that Jesus came to make all things new, to fill old forms and tired customs with new meaning. Jesus comes to do the same to this ancient institution, marriage, which is

destined to find new meaning in his name and presence
no matter how often it is betrayed, debased and cheap-
ened.

But there is something else. While Jesus is about his
business at the marriage in Cana, his mother Mary interferes, telling him when and what to do. Jesus' response is to dismiss her quite deliberately, making clear
that he is grown now, no longer her child, and intends
to be about his own business, thank you, in his own
good time.

So too with marriage. The man and the woman
step away from mothers and fathers to undertake their
own special work. Mary may watch her child, as many
another parent witnesses a child's marriage, but each
does so at a distance and with the full knowledge that
what occurs is the child's business. The work of parents,
as parents, has been completed.

*   *   *

. . . The marriage proposal came on a moonlit night in
late spring in the middle of a great field by a river. Their
joy was complete. Intentions clear, they rushed to wak-
en dear friends, even the priest who would officiate, to
proclaim the good news.

Not every one they awakened by telephone, however, responded with the same joyful enthusiasm. The
bride's mother, for one, was already becoming diffident
and demanding, withholding approval, making one last
bid to control her child, who now sought her own life
away from her mother's influence. Days and weeks passed. Each part of wedding planning was at issue for the
mother: the guest list, the place for the reception and the
menu, and more. Battle followed battle; the mother had

her way or else. Finally, it came to an impasse—over clothes. The groom's parents, as the hosts, held out for informal dress at the rehearsal dinner. Her mother refused to agree. They insisted. She threatened not to appear. The stakes escalated, and mother stated that she would cancel the wedding reception and remain at home for the entire event. All attempts at negotiation failed. The daughter made the only choice possible and was married in the absence of her mother, learning to her grief that marriage separates even as it unifies.

It signifies to us the mystery of the union between Christ and his Church, and Holy Scripture commends it to be honored among all people.

The union between this man and this woman is essentially a mystery. It is similar to the union between Christ—whose life, death and resurrection created the Church—and the Church—whose single task is to worship and proclaim her Christ. Christ and the Church —one cannot exist without the other. So it is with those who are married. The mystery of the union created in marriage is one of unparalleled intimacy and interdependence.

The most powerful statement which Holy Scripture makes in commending marriage are the words which conclude the second chapter of Genesis: "and they became one flesh." It is an insight of power and truth. The gift of becoming "one flesh" offered in marriage is a possibility beyond any other experience available to us—whether in friendship, child-bearing or any other form of human communion. While Jesus made clear that there are no marriages in heaven, for heaven is a quality of life beyond all we know here on earth, marriage is also as close as human beings may come to know the reality of heaven this side of the grave. To be at one with another human being, to be "one flesh" with a separate, distinct person, is to know that there is far more to human life than the prison of one's own skin. The miraculous is not a foreign state in which the rules of physics are overcome, but the infusion into daily life of the presence and possibility of God. It is precisely this which we know in the continuing moment that we become "one flesh" with the one who is beloved.

The ultimate symbol of being "one flesh" is the experience of orgasm, but this symbol, as does every symbol, participates in the entire reality which is marriage and never more than in moments of catastrophic, life-threatening illness.

*   *   *

. . . It was early on a rainy Wednesday morning when, after awakening in a strange town, they turned the car toward home, the final leg of their extended journey. From nowhere, without warning, he was struck with blinding and excrutiating pain in the forehead. He could not drive, he could not see, he could barely talk. The road stretched on through the dense growth of a southeastern plantation. Neither spoke. She sped, and then the great blue H appeared on the side of the road. One H led to another until they were there, struggling up the ramp into the Emergency Room.

They were left alone, as he lay on the examining room cot, whispering in that sterile and unknown place. Neither panicked, but each was convinced that this was it; he was going to die. But the issue really was not death, for in such a marriage death is not the issue; they had gone beyond that. The issue was parting. They realized that everything each of them had known and become in and through the other might end, and love, which is ever growing, never complete, would have to find a new form of expression through and beyond the grave.

"I love you," he said. She told him he shouldn't try to talk. "I love you," he said again. "Shh," she told him. "Save your strength. The doctor will be right along." "I don't want the doctor," he said, "I want you. I love you." He could not say it enough. "It hurts so much. I can't tell you how much it hurts. But somehow it only seems to hurt because I love you. If I didn't love you, there would not be any hurt because there wouldn't be anything. No feeling, just nothing. You are that feeling, and our love makes that possible. It makes everything possible."

It sounded as if he were rambling. But he wasn't, and she knew that. What came from within, through the pain, was his testimony to the abiding reality of the one thing which did remain as together they faced the reality of parting. That one thing remaining to them was the fact that they were "one flesh."

The union of husband and wife in heart, body and mind is intended by God

Marriage is a complete union, involving all there is of both persons. Holy Scripture suggests this begins with the creation of "one flesh." Nothing is to be reserved or held back from this commitment. Marriage is multi-dimensional: an emotional union, a physical union, and an intellectual and spiritual union. Two dimensions are flat, the third brings depth, form, substance and shape, while the fourth adds time, all we know of experience through history. In marriage each dimension becomes the marriage intended by God.

Once upon a time, the only advice parents offered children was: "Marriage is not a matter of 50%-50%. Not a bit. It is 90-90." They might as well have said that Toll House cookies are not the same without chocolate bits, or the car won't start if the ignition malfunctions. The old cliché that marriage will only work if each reserves a small corner of the self as private, never to be shared, is erroneous and worse, dangerous, for that small and reserved part will grow and grow and grow until it dominates the entire person and destroys the marriage.

*   *   *

. . . "My life is full, I mean, it's 'Go, Go, Go' all the time, twenty-four hours a day and seven days a week. There isn't even a moment most days to take a deep breath. And it's just the same for her. I mean we are busy people, making our way. What else can you expect? But listen, I understand. There's such a thing as quality time. That's what we reserve for each other, quality time. And when we're together, nothing interferes, nothing at all, pretty much. You know, unless something really crucial comes up, something which is absolutely necessary.

And the wife replied. "That's what he says. I think he really means it. God knows he's said it long enough and often enough. But it just doesn't work. Not for me anyway, not any more. I've had it, and I want out. When we were married, he was first and last a husband, and the most important thing was our marriage. That's what I mean to have. If it's not what he wants, then he can look elsewhere. He doesn't really want me to be his wife. I'm only a convenience, when it is convenient for him. That's not marriage."

for their mutual joy;

The first and most basic purpose of marriage is for each to offer the self in joy to the other. Joy comes first in this statement concerning the priorities and purpose of marriage—joy, not mutual aid, not primarily for the procreation of children. The claim is emphatically biblical: the essential fruit of marriage is the joy of becoming one flesh. That miracle has nothing whatever to do with children. It has to do with the unity of man and woman, who, in mutual joy, become husband and wife.

for the help and comfort given one another in prosperity and adversity;

Once the basic physical needs of food and shelter are served, and often even when they are not, then above all human beings need one another. We need to love and to be loved and to be saved from loneliness. The gift of marriage is the gift of one another. The gift of one another, standing together in help and support, in comfort and strength, embracing in times of laughter and in times of tears, embracing too when we are laughing through our tears and crying so desperately that laughter is the only antidote.

*   *   *

. . . Tears marked their marriage early. Less than a week after the ceremony, his father died. He had not died at the end of his life, but before his time was fulfilled. He had died no longer wishing to live alone, widowed, his children now far from home. He died only after his youngest child and only son had left home in order to marry. A few days before they had stood together, father and son, best man and groom, before the altar in the stone church on a bright and sunny June afternoon. The father had performed the final act with and for his child —the witnessing of marriage vows. Now he was gone, and all the times they might have shared together as friends and adults, together were gone too, forever. There was anguish, there was guilt, and there was deep, deep sorrow. All night long, or so it seemed, in the marriage bed they would share for years and years, he wept. But she was there to help and comfort in this first time of adversity. They knew that they were one flesh, now and forever.

and, when it is God's will, for the procreation of children

Children do not make a marriage, but they may make a family. The marriage exists before their arrival and after their departure and even if they do not arrive at all. They are the result of the marriage and would not exist without it, but they also exist apart from it. When and how they come, even with the wonders of contemporary fertility research and practise remains in great part a mystery.

*   *   *

. . . They had undertaken every kind of fertility test, followed careful procedures under the best medical supervision. Month followed month, the twenty-eight day cycle as regular and predictable as the finest Swiss watch. But still there was no child. Husband and wife endured one year, two years, three years, and they remained husband and wife, alone.

Her favorite aunt lay at home in bed at death's door, riddled with cancer. The young woman drove overnight to see her and say goodbye. Her aunt was weak but still had words to speak before death claimed her. What she said was this: "Your uncle and I have had a long and love-filled marriage. Our desire for children was always intense and never satisfied. Should this be your lot, my dear, remember your aunt and uncle who love you. Marriage prevails. Ours has been full and rich; yours will be too. God bless you."

Three days after the young woman returned to her husband, her aunt died. As preparations were being made for the trip to the funeral, she discovered that she was pregnant.

and their nurture in the knowledge and love of the Lord.

Should the marriage be blessed with children, these are a gift from God. They are entrusted to this man and this woman to be loved and nurtured in the name and honor of the giver. We come from the Lord and we go to the Lord. We are the Lord's. Our children belong to God. This they shall come to know and appreciate from their parents, those to whom they are entrusted for a brief span.

*   *   *

. . . She was the elder of his two step-children, still being formed, lovely, vulnerable in every way. She was loved, and she knew it, but she still had to make what she believed to be the most significant decision of her seventeen years: where to go to college. She did not want to make it alone.

She knew that neither of her natural parents could help her by responding objectively. The choice was between her father's small rural college and her mother's enormous state university. The choice itself required each to take a side, and the child did not want a contest, she wanted a decision, the right decision. And so she went to her stepfather, who was the one person she knew, right then, who could say to her, "Caroline, what is it that *you* want to do?" And when he asked that question, she knew her answer, and that was exactly what she did.

At the end of her freshman year, she took some time to be with her stepfather, to talk over the year with him. "I owe you a lot," she said. "This year has been really great. It never would have happened without you."

"You made it happen," he told her, "and you also made something wonderful happen for your mother and me."

Therefore marriage is not to be entered into unadvisedly or lightly, but reverently, deliberately,

St. Paul's admonition that marriage is the most significant choice any one of us will make in this lifetime has here been shortened and softened. Paul could not think of a great deal that was good to say about marriage, for he believed there was no time for it. The New Age would soon be upon us, and the world would come to an end, so there was little point in embarking on marriage. He was mistaken, and the world did not come to an end; nevertheless we continue to pay heed to his counsel. St. Paul makes it clear that marriage is the central and most important commitment a human being undertakes, marked by physical unity in the sexual act which makes two persons "one flesh," which, once undertaken, will never be undone.

and in accordance with the purposes for which it was instituted by God.

The Exhortation concludes as it began by stating emphatically that marriage is first and last God's creation, God's ordinance, God's business. Marriage transcends the romantic, the physical, the legal, the psychological, the intellectual. Marriage is set in the broadest and deepest dimension of all. Marriage belongs to God, and to enter into marriage is to enter into a quality of life and relationship in which God dwells. Marriage is a living embodiment of God's creation.

When a man and a woman appear before this altar, exchange vows, and become husband and wife, there and then a new being is created. That being is called forth by God and claimed by God. When human beings enter into marriage, a very daily, sometimes even humdrum existence, they become a part of the transcendent realm of God. God dwells in the midst of their marriage, sustaining and enlivening it in ways that we cannot imagine. Frederick Buechner has written that to be loved is an "ancient and most holy miracle. . . A miracle is when the whole is greater than the sum of its parts. A miracle is where one plus one equals a thousand." Marriage is a miracle. It is of God.

*   *   *

. . . The woman explained on national television that for the past five and a half years her husband, to whom she had been married for thirty-eight years, lay at home, immobile, unable to speak or to help himself in any way, the victim of a crippling stroke.

"Yet," she said, "it really is a joy to care for him, to feed and bathe him. While he can not speak, I am confident that he hears and recognizes me. It is difficult, however, to find the strength to turn him every two and a half hours."

"Where do you find the power, the courage to carry on this way, alone, and without apparent hope for these five and a half years?" the television host inquired.

"We are married."

THE BANNS

Into this holy union N. N. and   N. N. come now to be joined. If any of you can show just cause why they may not lawfully be married, speak now; or else for ever hold your peace.

The words stand alone, a kind of ancient embarrassment, whose only meaning seems to be bathos, melodrama, the moment for the former suitor, real or imaginary, to dash forward, seize his beloved, the bride, and carry her kicking and screaming from the church. They are our liturgical equivalent of the human appendix or the wisdom teeth. Once the banns served the useful purpose of official and even legal announcement of the forthcoming marriage, but now they are only a remembrance of times past.

The word "bann" means "proclamation." It was a formal announcement at a public service of worship of an intended marriage and existed in the days before the marriage license. Official permission for marriage was provided by the publication of the banns, which were repeated on three separate and successive occasions, con-

cluding with this, the final publication, just before the
marriage was actually to take place.

Melodramatic though they seem, the banns have
considerable impact. "Hear ye, hear ye," they seem to
say, "draw near and take careful note that this marriage
is now to take place." From that point the marriage begins. It is a new and inviolate thing, free from any kind
of intrusion or interference. Those who stand outside,
beyond this unity, are to remain outside, now and forever more. Failure to honor the bann will spell the failure of the marriage.

It is not always a former lover, however, who
threatens a marriage. The threat may come from those
closest to husband and wife, even from a mother or
father.

*   *   *

. . . A young and beautiful woman, born to wealth and
privilege, was the only daughter of a powerful father,
who commanded all in his sight and field of influence.
He indulged every whim of her life, and her radiant
beauty and easy smile revealed how accustomed she had
become to it. Always she had received everything her
heart desired. So when she first caught sight of him on
the college campus—tall and blonde, more handsome
than a youthful Robert Redford—she wanted him for
her very own.

They were married very shortly following graduation to live happily ever after, or for as long as the
young man could make the grade. Daddy was not about
to let go, not until his child had everything she had always wanted, everything which he had always provided.
But how could this happen? The young man was set on

living a life of purpose and meaning, pursuing his
childhood dream of housing and feeding the homeless.
This, they all agreed, was a noble endeavor, but not quite
the right thing for *her* husband.

The pressure was on. Subtle at first, it was expressed
as embarrassment, a few comments about the manliness
of power and prestige, a touch of ridicule. Soon the
pressure was stronger, expressed in outright scorn,
which was neither subtle nor polite. Finally, there was
rejection. "Don't return home again, Princess, as long as
you are married to him."

And so the young man left his work for the
homeless, lost his vision, and devoted his life to making
peace by making money.

Often I cried because I could not bend
your will to mine, because you would not be
that which my thought found fair, nor would you lend
yourself to fostering the child in me;
nor would you be my child for any ease
or comfort that might promise to your mind;
nor would you love but to be loved, nor seize
your right to tell me where I had been blind. . . .

THE CHARGE

*I require and charge you both, here in the presence of
God, that if either of you know any reason why you may
not be united in marriage lawfully, and in accordance
with God's Word, you do now confess it.*

These words are spoken only to the man and
woman. They are as private as they are powerful, and

this is the intention. Several themes run through this entire ceremony, and none is more important than the claim that marriage is a serious life-long affair, undertaken under clear and strong conditions. The responsibility for the marriage involves others: the witnesses, the Church, the priest, the parents, the gathered company. But the greatest burden of responsibility clearly falls upon the persons who have come here to be married. That is what the charge says. It then goes on to imply all of the conditions which create biblical, Christian marriage: it is lifelong, it is monogamous, it is singular and it is single-minded.

The demand is a compelling one. It is asking that the marriage be perfect—"perfect" in the sense that it be whole, without seam. There shall be no separate, private part which is reserved from this commitment, these vows, and there shall be no duress of any kind.

*   *   *

. . . The two met during the very first weeks of college. Everything about the new friendship was exciting. Different in background and experience, they were bound together in common interests and concerns, and they stimulated one another in this new and far freer form of relationship in ways neither of them had ever known.

They spent more and more time together. Virginal, cautious, still more than once they found themselves in the same bed. Suddenly, they said that they were never quite sure how it happened, she was pregnant. An over-the-counter drug store kit gave them the news. They were excited, and they were also aghast. Freshman year was not even over, and a long life lay ahead for each. What should they do?

After long conversations and many sleepless nights, he convinced her to go with him to a friend of the family whom he had always trusted.

After they had told their story, the friend said :

"I will not tell you what to do. This is a choice which you have to make, and I shall happily sit here with you for as long as you like, talking over the various choices with you. One thing, and one thing only, I shall tell you. Under no circumstance whatsoever are you to be married. This would be to marry under duress, however carefully it is masked and concealed. That would never be right.

Marriage is a single-minded, lifelong commitment that I doubt you are ready to make, let alone to think about. As you grow in age and grace and wisdom, it may well be that this is what you will each desire—marriage to one another. When this happens, if it is to succeed, all the conditions must be as perfect as human beings are able to manage. This is not your present condition."

. . . if either of you know any reason why you may not be united in marriage . . . you do now confess it.

Marriage is never an easy undertaking, even when love is hot and fresh and romantic and new. It requires more than either the man or the woman has ever invested in any other person or undertaking. So it must occur under conditions that are whole, perfect, with no reservation and nothing withheld, now or in the future. Nothing at all may be allowed to stand between those about to affirm their mutual life-long commitment before God.

THE DECLARATION OF CONSENT

N., will you have this man to be your husband; to live together in the covenant of marriage?
N., will you have this woman to be your wife; to live together in the covenant of marriage?

These opening words contain the declaration of intention, or betrothal. In an earlier time, when customs were in some ways similar to what many now believe are new patterns, if a couple decided to marry, they visited the local parish church to celebrate their betrothal, the declaration of their intention to be married. Then they departed to test its feasibility. After living together, if marriage still seemed a good idea, they returned to the local parish church to exchange marriage vows. The proof that marriage was a good idea was often pregnancy, for this was a time when many children were an economic necessity in the family to help with the work. In the fifteenth century, the Flemish artist, Van Eyck, immortalized such a couple in his famous work, "The Betrothed," which shows a man and woman standing before a window, obviously much in love, just as the young woman is very obviously pregnant. So the fairly common contemporary practice of couples "living together" to test the viability of marriage is hardly a new invention. Yet keep in mind that the betrothal is a firm and very specific commitment, while many varieties of trial marriage contain so many conditions as to make any lasting marriage impossible.

Will you love him,
Will you love her,

The verb to love is central to the entire adventure of marriage; its reality remains a constant. Yet we are

handicapped by not really knowing what we mean by it.
The word is overused, misunderstood, or used with no
substance and little meaning. More than one couple, on
approaching parents or priest or even close friends to
discuss marriage, when asked exactly why they want to
marry this particular person are apt to blurt out, "Why?
Because I love her! That's why." Then there is silence.
And if no one bails him out, more silence, which grows
into deeper and deeper embarrassment until at long last
he manages to get out, "I just can't explain."

*   *   *

. . . The young woman called her parents in the dark and
early hours of Monday morning with the exciting news
that he had just proposed, and she had accepted. Words
poured out, tears flowed, but even in all the excitement,
or perhaps because of it, when he came on the phone, he
had words to say to them, precise and definite words. "I
want you to know why I love your daughter! We all
know she is wonderful, but she is wonderful because she
is honest, she cares about things and people that you and
I know matter. And she is so emotional. How I love her
highs and her lows. She lives all of her life, every moment of every day, with a joy and a spirit which has
changed my life and I can never be without it." He
spoke quickly, with clarity and conviction. His was a
love which knew both language and a person, and it
sharpened and deepened his commitment.

*   *   *

Much of the difficulty we all experience in knowing
what is meant by the word "love" is caused by the pov-

erty of our language, which has only one word to describe feelings for ice cream, my country, or my beloved. This just will not do. The Greek language has four words for our one, and each means something different; love as we know it in marriage includes all four.

The first is affection, the most basic love, a part of every love, and no love is possible without it. Affection is built upon familiarity, time spent together, time which binds two persons together in common experience. A frequent reason many couples give for their continued commitment in marriage is "shared history," an irreplaceable gift built through years of life together.

The second is friendship. A relationship moves from the familiarity of affection to the desire to develop common bonds, common understandings, common hopes and dreams. Friends are those with whom we share more than time; a friendship is born when we discover that someone else has the same perception, same orientation, same interests. Friends are those who understand what we are thinking and feeling without being told.

The third is eros, sexual passion. It is not lust, which is blind. Eros seeks one particular person and one person only, striving for fusion with that other through physical expression. Eros will not occur unless first one has experienced affection and then friendship.

The fourth is agape, the love of God. It makes demands but sets no conditions. It is love which sees and knows us just as we are and loves us still and all. Agape is beyond human possibility, yet in marriage a relationship created by God and surrounded by grace, it may happen. Agape is one glimpse, perhaps the only one we shall ever have in this life, of the depth and reality of God's love.

Marriage includes all four loves. To survive, it must be richly blessed with eros and agape, yet before these can endure and prevail, there must be familiarity and friendship.

*   *   *

. . . The separation of summer had ended, and a small group gathered to share stories and reclaim the threads of their friendship. The first to share an important memory stood to speak, handsome, articulate and polished. His words reached out and touched each one of them deeply as he recounted an experience of August, when he and his "closest" friend walked the long white beach and discovered a dramatically new level of communication. It was immediately and disturbingly clear that this best friend was not his wife. In that realization, right then, there could be no doubt in anyone's mind that the marriage had ended. Six months later that announcement was made to the world.

comfort him,
comfort her,

The original meaning of comfort is to strengthen. It is possible within marriage for each to make the other feel good, but what is needed far more is a source of strength and uplift. The world provides us with more battles than we need. Within the marriage bond, we stand together to be strengthened with, for, and by the other.

honor and keep him,
honor and keep her,

The idea of "honor" suggests worship. It is close to prayer. If we are to be married, then we hold our spouse in esteem, ascribing high value to the beloved whom we honor with our life and whole being. "Keep," on the other hand, means more than merely hanging on, it is to embrace the other with complete and total fidelity.

Two old friends were driving home together after the first lunch they had had with each other in years. They were discussing marriage and talked about what could happen in marriage when both spouses are faithful to their vows, when each "keeps" to the other. There was a reflective silence, and then the words: "I wish I could describe the ecstasy which continues to grow as our marriage unfolds." More silence, and the reply, "You're right. It's the only thing that works."

in sickness and in health;

We know why these words are there, and we know what they mean, and we avoid them in every way we can. Health is easy. Health means wholeness and well-being and happiness. Health is the reason we chose to be married in the first place. Health does not present a demand, only an opportunity.

Sickness is another question. Sickness brings separation and distance and difficulty, as well as a host of conditions for which no one ever bargains. In sickness there is simply not the same quality of marriage and relationship as in health. One person is broken; both are alone. The challenge even of a bad bout of flu is not easy, but what if the illness is crippling? What if it is totally debilitating, changing my spouse into someone completely different from the person I am marrying? That is just the point. If we intend to be married, then we intend to maintain that marriage in every condition, and to enable it to grow and flourish in every kind of circumstance.

*   *   *

. . . The cancer began in her ear. Treatments did not curb
the spread to the jaw bone until the sickness was all
through the right side of her face, threatening her brain,
her very life.   Only massive and destructive surgery
might help, but its success was doubtful. The surgeons
proceeded, removing half of her face. Reconstruction, if
possible, would have to wait for several years. Hos-
pitalization lasted weeks.

He ran the house alone, not that he was much use
in the hospital. Even as she lay in her hospital bed,
when the bandages were at long last removed, he
discovered he could not bear to look upon what was
now a caricature of the face he had once loved. In his
pain and aloneness he fed, comforted and seduced
himself into loving the neighbor just down the street.
When his wife finally overcame her sickness and
returned, healthy, from the hospital, their marriage had
ended.

*and, forsaking all others, be faithful to him as long as
you both shall live?*
*and, forsaking all others, be faithful to her as long as you
both shall live?*

I will.

G. K. Chesterton, prolific apologist for the Christian
faith, once constructed a myth, the story of an idyllic
tropical isle in which all was perfection and bliss. There
was, however, one restriction, which the inhabitants of
this place must observe to preserve the peace and order
of an island where the sun always shone by day, and rain

fell only at night, and food was provided without any human labor by the rich tropical vegetation. There had been built, long years ago, a great barrier wall, which stood all along the edge of the beach, separating land and sea. The restriction was that this wall should never be removed. While the great wall stood, life proceeded peacefully and calmly from one generation to another.

At last there arose a vigorous younger generation, who were offended by this great wall. They decided to take the life of their community in their own hands and remove this obstruction of their view of the sea; one unusually dark night, they took down the wall. The next morning when the sun arose, so too did a great wind, which increased to greater and greater strength, and whipped the ocean beyond the beach to an unimaginable ferocity. When the day had ended, virtually the entire island, its inhabitants and all their dwellings and marks of civilization had been removed forever.

Chesterton provides, in fanciful but believable form, a vivid description of complete and total fidelity. Chesterton makes it very clear that human life may only be lived within certain carefully defined limits. These limits are created through fidelity. Each person must make choices and then be faithful to those choices, living within the boundaries the choices have created. This is fidelity, and fidelity is the cornerstone and foundation of any human relationship—most especially marriage.

Now we two stand midway upon our road
and strive to fathom what we have become
since our first tributary courses flowed
in a single channel. Cautiously, we plumb
our deepened waters to discern what now
is yours, what mine, but we have merged so long

there is no human judgment can allow
what each to each henceforward can belong.
Though yours may be the waters that run deep
and mine the surface eddies and the foam
that cries against the rocks, our lives must keep
their common course through cliffs or yielding loam.
I am borne upon your depths and you must share
forever my affinity for air.

It is a moment to pause. The first major work is complete. The woman and man have said to all assembled: "We are ready to marry." Even as they are ready, it is now time to ask: "Is there anyone out there? Are you listening?   What have you to offer to those of us who are to marry?"
The priest then turns to the congregation and asks:

Will all of you witnessing these promises do all in your power to uphold these two persons in their marriage?

The people reply:

We will.

Before this all words addressed to the congregation have contained prohibitions: "or forever hold your peace . . . forsaking all others . . . let no one put asunder." Here we have a demand. Everyone present is asked to be involved, actively and positively, in this union. Each person is more than a witness. All are participants now and in the future, especially in the future, and vow to play their part in strengthening and upholding this marriage. For marriage is not merely a private affair. It is a public act, which involves throughout its life many other people. With these words the witnesses are re-

minded and commanded that the care involved in upholding this marriage is daily, devoted, and constant.

*   *   *

. . . There were only a few members of the class, twenty
at most, who had chosen to attend their twenty-fifth reunion. Once upon a time they had known each other
well; the depth of involvement and intimacy had been
real. It was gone now, but they had gathered in its name
and memory.

The reunion had been full of eating and drinking,
with happy and superficial conversation. Now, before
they parted, it was time for serious business. They gathered in a large circle in a private room and began to
speak, one at a time, of what had been most important
in the years since they had been together. The stories
were not of success, but of pain. Each life had borne its
share. Some had borne more than others, and all more
than had been deserved.

The pain centered particularly on marriage. The
final story was the most eloquent. Without a word of
warning, as the story was remembered and told, the
man, an Episcopal priest, had returned one day in the
fifteenth year of their marriage to find his wife packed
and ready to leave him for another man. The shock he
had felt then was apparent in his numbness even as he
spoke. There was silence after his story, and in the silence, he pronounced his own benediction. "I guess it's
not easy to be a priest and to be married." Again, there
was silence, and through it someone who was wiser
said, "It's not easy to be married."

*   *   *

It is not easy to be married, just as, all too often, it is not easy to be alive. The richness of the experience, however, is all the more precious as marriage is supported and upheld by the friends who surround it. For as each marriage works out its salvation with fear and trembling in the presence of friends, who believe that marriage is the primary good, then the marriage will be upheld. The age of the lonely individual, born of the fear, mistrust and betrayal which pervaded the 1960's, has moved even into marriage, the most intimate of all institutions, and caused great havoc. The promise of the witnesses asserts that their presence demands more than assent, it requires involvement and forthright, even blatant, support.

*   *   *

. . . The night was bitterly cold, the sky ablaze with the light of every star, and the powerful northwest wind, which had swept through during the day, had died. Stillness everywhere emphasized the crackling "crunch, crunch" of stiff snow underfoot. It was late, close to ten, and the work of the evening finished, when for some inexplicable reason he was drawn out of the house and into the night. Walking up the street, as if he knew where he was going, he knocked on the door of some good friends. Many was the time when one couple or the other had been present for a turning point through the years of both marriages, his and theirs. Somehow, now, he felt that he had to be with them. Giving a casual excuse as they opened the door and let him in, the three friends gathered about the living room fire, now only a glow of coals.

As they talked of this and that, he began to wonder, "Why am I here? What am I supposed to do? It just doesn't make much sense to drop in for a chat at this time of night." The telephone rang, and the husband went out to the kitchen to answer. Minutes went by. He was gone too long. They began to wonder if they should drop their pretense of conversation and just listen, when suddenly, it was unnecessary.

"Bob, just what the hell are you trying to tell me? Are you saying that my job of twenty years is gone, just like that? I'm supposed to work for that son of a bitch! You can keep your god damn job!" He slammed down the telephone.

They went into the kitchen together. "I guess you heard it all." Nods. Silence. They started to pray. First, each alone, in silence. Then, one by one, they clasped one another's hands and began to say the Lord's Prayer. The husband put his head in his hands and wept, partly with rage.

It was even later when he rose to go. Handshakes, kisses, thanks. He walked home not certain if his presence had made a difference in the outcome, only knowing that when marriage faces a test, it is good to know you are not alone.

*   *   *

. . . Their second marriage was to be quietly performed with only a handful of family members present, no one else. Eight good friends, however, knew that they had to be present and came uninvited. Marriage requires witnesses who care and are committed to continuing support.

After this, the friendships between the couples flourished, grew in the good times of laughter and the pain of shared tears. Common bonds became stronger. The bonds created trust. Trust invites test.

The test came just at dinner time one evening, when the still newly married couple called to say they would not be coming to the meal planned for four. Life was too much for them, too full, they had been fighting for two days. "We would not be good guests. Let's make it another time." Click. Their friends, however, knew there was no other time. This was the time. They packed the dinner up, chose some wine and, food in hand, along with funny hats and masks, went to join their friends. If conflict keeps the guests from friendship, they told each other, friendship, even if unwelcome, will join them in conflict. And so it happened. When the evening ended, nothing was resolved, but soon it would be. Their marriage vows were not theirs alone.

*   *   *

The life of this witness begins with the response, "We will," and extends as far into the future of that marriage as "will" allows and demands. The opportunities are boundless, since the continued health of the marriage is partly in the care of the witnesses.

The creation of a marriage, together with the support which   strengthens that creation, are among the most significant opportunities anyone knows. Such opportunities occur at unpredictable moments—at times unwelcome, their outcome uncertain. Nor is this support easy to offer; it is hard to know what is acceptable, what is needed, what is necessary. But support will be

offered.   Otherwise the witnesses had best never have
stated their promise, "We will."

*   *   *

. . . They had known one another from childhood.   Parents, grandparents and all the members of their family
supported this passionate union, full of emotion,
though of little substance. Fervor and sexual passion
sustained them in the first chaotic years of navy travel
and then heedless career change, years in which three
children were quickly born. The more the demands of
the marriage grew, the more distracted he became, and
he found it necessary to be frequently away on business.
The more he was away, the more other men gathered,
drawn by her. He became more and more distant, she
more sensual. The result was inevitable. Soon she was
with child—not his.

Separation was immediate, marked first by letters,
then calls and visits. Divorce seemed inevitable, but they
were still passionately in love. Dismayed by what had
happened, unable to understand, they remained desperate, vulnerable. In their need, they reached out to the
friends who had witnessed their vows as they had also
witnessed their downfall.

Driving down the street one morning, he saw a
bumper sticker: "You are a miracle." He said to himself,
"That's true, you know. But no miracle ever took place
in a vacuum." He took a U Turn, right there,   and
made his way to the house where she then lived, alone,
with their children. Taking the stairs, two at a time, he
had no idea what he might say if she even opened the
door. She did, halfway. "Could I come in for a minute?"
The living room was in chaos; signs of his children were

everywhere. He felt a terrible loneliness, and he wanted
to touch her, to stop the thing that was happening, but
he was helpless, trapped in its momentum. He wanted
to tell her that they were a miracle, he and she, but he
didn't have the courage.

They sat in silence for what seemed like hours—it
was thirty minutes. Finally, he got up from the couch
and began to dial frantically, calling their best man, who
was one of his oldest and dearest friends. "We need you.
Come over, now, please, you must, hurry." He came and
his wife came with him. Together the four sat and talked
and talked—all morning and into the afternoon. Good
friends sensed all that was happening and knew how to
say for him those words which he had been unable to
speak. Distances closed and differences diminished.
Night came. They were not finished. Exhausted, they
agreed to part for the night and come together again at
daybreak. A marriage was born, not for the second time,
but for the first.

*   *   *

Every marriage is fragile, often in danger of
breaking. When things become unraveled, and the fabric
of the tapestry tears apart, those right in its very midst,
husband and wife, are physically unable to perform the
necessary mending. Each is unable to be Christ to the
other; each is unable even to be one's self to the other.
At just such a time there must be other voices, other
hands, who provide the grace and the gift which will
save the marriage for that day and many more. Those
voices and those hands belong to the witnesses, real and
symbolic, who stood with that husband and that wife on

their wedding day, when it all began, and joined their voices together with the words, "We will."

ONE FLESH

THE MINISTRY OF THE WORD

The man and the woman stand before God, brought by their own intention, supported by witnesses. Yet there is more to this moment. The "more" is the heritage of Holy Scripture, older than this liturgy. Scripture proclaims that marriage is one way each of us, male and female, has been called by God to live—called in creation, called in Christ, called in our life for one another.

The marriage rite of the Prayer Book is rooted in a biblical view of the world and of sexuality. This perspective, developed through the ages, has been delivered to us from our ancestors in terms precise and challenging. The images from Scripture, in the readings which follow, are the very ground in which our lives are to be rooted and from which we shall grow into the fullness of grace to which God calls us.

Set in the context of the Eucharist, the biblical readings include an Old Testament Lesson and an Epistle, to be read by friends or members of the family, and a Gospel. Five possibilities are suggested for each and from these a selection can be made. The tone throughout is created by the wedding collect.

O gracious and everliving God, you have created us male and female in your image: Look mercifully upon this man and this woman who come to you seeking your blessing, and assist them with your grace, that with

*true fidelity and steadfast love they may honor and keep
the promises and vows they make; through Jesus Christ
our Savior, who lives and reigns with you in the unity
of the Holy Spirit, one God, for ever and ever. Amen.*

The Ministry of the Word is introduced with this
collect, which sets marriage in the context of our creation
by God in his image, a reference to the creation of man
and woman in the first chapter of Genesis.

Human life exists as a whole in two parts, male and
female, made in the image of God. Each of us, therefore,
has the potentiality to be perfect, to be whole, to be one
—as male and female bound together in
marriage—"one flesh."

The collect further describes this potential in terms
of two essential polarities that create a tension, the
tension within which marriage lives and grows.

The first polarity is human choice. Marriage is both
what we intend and what we actually create. Marriage is
always the result of a self-fulfilling prophecy. What we
mean to achieve within the context of marriage is
precisely what happens. Time and time again, when
long and well married people are asked why their
marriage was possible, they answer, "It was what we
intended. We worked to create it and to maintain and
preserve it." The myth of romantic love is a powerful
myth, but it is not a foundation for enduring marriage.

Marriage that does not prevail ends, finally, for one
reason and one reason only: the spouses involved did
not intend the marriage to prevail. The choices which
human beings make within the context of marriage are
the choices which determine their destiny. This power

of choice is also what it means to be "made in the image
of God."

*   *   *

. . .Walking to the edge of the parking area, standing by
his own old car, he looked off at the beautiful ranks of
mountains, their contours bare in winter clarity,
accented by the snow on the upper slopes. He tried for a
moment to imagine them with tourist eyes, or as Jean
and he had seen them when they first moved to the
state three years ago and constantly exclaimed over its
scenic loveliness. Now they had become background, as
everything does in habituation. It is hard to continue to
see beauty; hard to continue to feel zest; hard to continue
to feel love. It is a devotion, an act of will to see freshly
each day, to say *look!* with a renewed wonder; to fling
oneself into familiar experience, to cast off distraction
and say *beloved.* . . .

*   *   *

The second polarity is God's grace. Marriage is set on
course by our own choice, but it will only survive in the
power of God's grace. Grace is gift. Grace is never
deserved, never earned. Grace is not frequently experienced, yet without it, life is impossible. Grace is the
moment when the other says, "I love you," and you
know full well that there is nothing lovable about you.
Grace is the moment when another says "Thank you,"
when you were only trying to serve yourself. Grace is
the moment when at the same time it seems that you
really do truly matter to someone else, when it is clear

that you do not matter to yourself. Grace is the ethos,
the magic, the reality which surrounds a marriage and
allows it to live and breathe and stretch and flourish.
Grace is the unbelievable experience of living in the
midst of a miracle, when one plus one really does equal
a thousand. Grace is far beyond the world of contract
and agreement and the tie that binds. Without grace
marriage is impossible.

Two polarities: choice and grace. They are opposites,
and they create a tension, the tension in which marriage
lives and grows.

*   *   *

. . . One bright and sunny autumn Sunday some years
ago a young preacher delivered a passionate sermon on
the theme of mutual responsibility and interdependence. It was part of the Anglican Communion's
campaign to strengthen common bonds throughout the
Christian Church, with global, national, and personal
implications. He told his congregation that unless they
undertook mutual responsibility and interdependence
for those whom they could reach out and touch, then
there would be no wider impact. When the service was
over one of the ushers, while passing through the pews,
found a service leaflet on which was written: "Did I tell
you this morning that you look lovely?"

THE OLD TESTAMENT LESSON

"Then the Lord God took the man and put him in the
garden of Eden to till it and keep it. And the Lord God

commanded the man, saying, "You may eat freely of every tree of the garden; but of the tree of the knowledge of good and evil you shall not eat, for in the day that you eat of it you will die."

Then the Lord God said, "It is not good that man should be alone; I will make him a helper fit for him." So out of the ground the Lord God formed every beast of the field and every bird of the air, and brought them to the man to see what he would call them; and whatever the man called every living creature, that was its name. The man gave names to all cattle, and to the birds of the air, and to every beast of the field; but for the man there was not found a helper fit for him. So the Lord God caused a deep sleep to fall upon the man, and while he slept he took one of his ribs and closed up its place with flesh; and the rib which the Lord God had taken from the man he made into a woman and brought her to the man. Then the man said,

This at last is bone of my bones
and flesh of my flesh;
she shall be called Woman,
because she was taken out of
Man.

Therefore a man leaves his father and his mother and cleaves to his wife, and they become one flesh."

GENESIS 2:15-24

Genesis contains two quite separate accounts of the creation. This story, from the second chapter of Genesis, is by far the more ancient of the two and is included in this liturgy for at least two reasons. First, it makes quite clear, but from a different point of view, the relationship between human nature and God. Human beings are set apart. This important biblical reality places marriage in its necessary, sacred, and unavoidable context. Second, the passage concludes with a most astounding biblical insight regarding the nature of marriage: marriage is a new, different form of the created order, the reality of one flesh.

Soon after her engagement, our eldest daughter asked, half in jest, "What is the most important part of marriage?" The answer—also half in jest—"Sex!"—is at the same time quite untrue and totally accurate—a paradox.

Every sacrament is marked by physical expression. In marriage that is sexual intercourse, the outward and visible sign of an inward and spiritual grace. Sexual expression within the context of marriage is thus the outward expression of the reality which exists within the union. Sex is the expression of a profound and unusual order of relationship. Sex does not create the relationship, but results from it. Sex is the marriage eucharist—dissolving tensions, producing harmony, and giving a real sense of the spiritual unity of life and love.

The sacrament of marriage is expressed in sexual intercourse; these two profound realities—marriage and sexual intercourse—are integral. As one ceases to exist, so will the other. This reality is as predictable as the moment of sunrise, yet it is also clear that this understanding runs contrary to contemporary practice, which makes sexual intercourse a commodity.

If then a marriage is to remain alive and vital and growing, so must the sexual relationship. A dead marriage will be dead sexually. Yet the absence of sex does not kill the marriage, it merely confirms the fact of death. Unless the sexual expression of the marriage bond is fed and nourished and allowed to prosper, then the marital bond itself will fail and die from lack of nourishment. The Bible is as accurate here as it can be. The glory and goodness of sex are celebrated, hallowed, proclaimed—not merely for its   power to recreate the species, but also as the means by which a man and a woman become one flesh.

The reality of one flesh is the experience of the marriage bed, both in the very act of sexual intercourse, and in the experience of sleeping, not alone, but wrapped together. When marriage partners move first into separate beds, and then into separate bedrooms, the union is in peril. No doubt it ended long ago and continues now only in appearance. The experience of one flesh can not transcend single beds or walls of plaster.

*   *   *

. . . Earlier in the marriage, it was physical passion which would stir one or the other. Hardly ever wakening from the embrace in which they had originally found sleep, they would unite, deep within, bone to bone, almost frantic, furious, with enormous release and the deepest kind of wordless communion. It was occasioned by the sexual, then transformed   into a new dimension of spiritual union, which would fill the next day with peace.

Later, it was not passion but terror which interrupted the subdued consciousness of sleep. The night terrors, everyone has them, she always said, strike in the dark absence of light and vigor and bring an overwhelming sensation of loneliness. Suddenly, wide awake, terrified in the dark, arms reach out to embrace, to hold, to seek comfort. Then there is talk, sometimes for two hours or more, talk that unites soul to soul, bone to bone.

*   *   *

The time spent asleep is a part of the time of each day given to the married couple to spend together. It is a time of special and very often profound communication.

By a curious route this subject arose in a very personal conversation with a friend and professional colleague. Someone had pointed out to him that he could always create additional time in the day simply by rising earlier. My friend said that for him this was impossible. "For the past twenty years I doubt that I have ever spent an evening alone with my wife, but she places one inviolable condition on our marriage; whenever she is in bed, we are to be there together. Her custom is to retire promptly and sleep for eight hours. Rising at five would be out of the question."

The reality of one flesh extends beyond the marriage bed into every aspect of married life, while the total unity of man and woman in marriage finds its final symbol and expression in sexual intercourse. It does not matter which is cause and which effect. What does matter is that the creation of marriage is rooted and expressed in the overpowering experience of one flesh, two persons united as one in mind, body and spirit.

*   *   *

. . . The mark of their relationship was intercourse, intercourse of all kinds. Mind to mind, spirit to spirit, they spoke to one another with and without words, although words were largely essential. Yet often, daily, one would answer a question which had never been asked, only formed in the mind of the other. Or one would begin a conversation at mid-point or continue it, leaving unspoken great segments of commentary and argument. They spoke frequently of being inside the head of the other, and able to move from one being to another.

It has been said that no one can know what it means to be truly inside the skin of another. But for those who are married and have become one flesh, a greater, mystical union enfolds both.

We might unsay the marriage vows we said,
dissolve the legal ties and sign our names
to documents of disunion, go our ways,
proclaim to all the world we were unwed,
from thence then sleep virginal in narrow bed,
dwell hemispheres apart, seek separate graves,
walk individual all our mortal days,
each to the other live as to one dead.
Yet never from my heart could I erase
the shape it has taken lying next your heart.
My thought is half your own, your tears half mine.
I am formed upon your bone. Time's silent art
has etched your hours of sorrow on my face,
has sealed my speech with your indelible sign.

THE EPISTLE

"If I speak with the tongues of men and of angels, but have not love, I am a noisy gong or a clanging cymbal. And if I have prophetic powers, and understand all mysteries and all knowledge, and if I have all faith, so as to remove mountains, but have not love, I am nothing. If I give away all I have, and if I deliver my body to be burned, but have not love, I gain nothing.

Love is patient and kind; love is not jealous or boastful; it is not arrogant or rude. Love does not insist on its own way; it is not irritable or resentful; it does not rejoice at wrong, but rejoices in the right. Love bears all things, believes all things, hopes all things, endures all things."

I CORINTHIANS 13: 1-7

St. Paul's great hymn to love is not ostensibly speaking of marriage at all, but of the quality of love Christians express, one to another, as members of the body of Christ. This is the love which grows from God's unbounded love in Christ. This is the love which creates marriage, the community of two in whose presence Christ dwells. When Jesus promised to be in our midst "whenever two or three are gathered together," he was speaking not of a minimum, but a maximum expectation. One unit in which Jesus dwells is marriage. It is a marriage which may grow into a family, both immediate and extended, but the love is rooted and first grows in marriage.

The intimate communion of marriage offers powerful opportunities to succomb to temptation and wound the spouse who has become open and vulnerable. If we can think the thoughts of our husband and wife even before they occur, if we know that other through and through, there is no end to the pain which we can inflict. The curious power of the love of the marriage bond, however, does not need to insist on its own way. Rather, it has the power through grace to look beyond itself to find fulfillment in the beloved.

If this love is not arrogant, it enables the married person to transcend self within marriage. Marriage is a state that exists outside and alongside both partners, while embracing them. Such love is patient and kind, just as it is not jealous or boastful or arrogant or rude; it has no need to be. The exercise of destructive power takes its toll on both. The power that infuses this love is able to bear all things, believe all things, hope all things, and endure all things—only because the power of this love comes from beyond itself, through Christ, and in every present moment is the incarnation of Christ in that marriage.

*   *   *

. . . Difficult as most would find it to believe, it was true: both of them were virgins. Their wedding night was fulfilling, although it certainly left ample room for improvement. The possibility of improvement was exciting, to be sure, just as long as it continued. Even in their most honest moment neither could complain. But intimacy takes time, sometimes it took more time than either really wanted to give. It also took privacy, sometimes more than living in their parents' house made available. It took openness and increasing knowledge and a good deal of patience.

In the slow and sometimes painful stages of learning about one another, they acquired deep personal knowledge, which could not be learned from books or films or even conversation. Their familiarity produced his willingness to care more for her than for himself, and her realization that the greatest moments of orgasmic fulfillment came from hard-won intimacy. Technique came with time and practice but mostly from the willingness to be with and for one another.

*   *   *

Christ's life and death were his "liturgy," his work, offered on our behalf. As Christ offered himself, so it is made possible for each of us to subject ourselves, one to another, in his name and love. This establishes a standard for all human relationships, most especially marriage.

The standard is one of sacrifice ("to make holy"), offering which is total, entire, open and complete. The standard is mutual subjection—to place oneself under the other, wholly vulnerable. By these standards, in the name and love of Christ, we are to be with and for one another.

We offer ourselves to our spouse and are known, fully, and accepted and loved, even as we ourselves love the other in the marriage bond. This knowledge leads to acceptance. It is not acceptance of what we might wish to be, but of who we actually are. Such acceptance is once and for all, the very foundation of marriage. It is grace in all its fullness. Such acceptance results in a sense of worth, self-worth, which is given by the one to the other. Somehow this makes it possible to mean something, be something, even do something. Every moment, every word, every action suddenly come into being in a new way. Strange and wonderful, quite mysterious, one is unable to function fully without the other. The ancient and most holy miracle: to be loved. One plus one equals a thousand.

Willingness to sacrifice for the beloved, and vulnerability, willingness to stand before one another naked and unashamed, result in interdependence. The interdependence of Christian marriage is a model for all human relationships. Two partners must be willing and able to stand quite apart as functioning human beings, fully capable of living a full life independent of one another. Yet they are totally unwilling to do so. Each chooses to see life as only and fully possible as each draws strength and sustenance and joy through and from the other. This is interdependence. Every moment, every word, every action are finally only made possible for each by the other.

*   *   *

. . . Neither could ever say when and how their love really first began. The love of hot, sexual passion had begun at the very beginnning, never to go away. They wondered about the deeper, abiding, love, which gave full knowledge, one of the other. When did that kind of love start? Not before marriage, certainly. No, it was many, many years later. It just grew. Yet they also knew it had always been there, from that first moment of deep, abiding friendship. It began with friendship, hours of shared dreams and plans and memories, hours that had no single point of beginning and went on and on.

Through it all, there was nothing she did not know of him, nor he of her. Weird habits, strange tastes, curious memories—qualities mysterious, even disliked in others, are seen as part of that person whom I know and love. What each understood and loved about the other was everything that was there. And all of it was right there, all of the time.

The result: common hopes, common memories, common dreams.

Love is not gazing in another's eyes,
finding another fair, nor being found,
not tenderness to hush another's cries,
nor strength that lifts one, fallen, from the ground.
Love is two faces set toward one star
that two who see may mark as their own north,
and set their course by it however far
their separate paths may wander back and forth.

THE GOSPEL

The Ministry of the Word, introduced by the collect, offers the perspective of Holy Scripture to the celebration and blessing of this marriage. The Old Testament lesson spoke specifically of the biblical nature of the marriage bond of one flesh. The Epistle describes the nature of Christian love and sacrifice within the bond of marriage. Now the Gospel will announce the Good News of Christ to be proclaimed by this marriage to the world in which it will live.

"Seeing the crowds, he went up on the mountain, and when he sat down his disciples came to him. And he opened his mouth and taught them, saying:

Blessed are the poor in spirit, for theirs is the kingdom of heaven.
Blessed are those who mourn, for they shall be comforted.
Blessed are those who hunger and thirst for righteousness, for they shall be satisfied.
Blessed are the merciful, for they shall obtain mercy.
Blessed are the pure in heart, for they shall see God.
Blessed are the peacemakers, for they shall be called the sons of God.
Blessed are those who are persecuted for righteousness' sake, for theirs is the kingdom of heaven."

- MATTHEW 5:1-10

These words are addressed to the chosen few. When Jesus gave the Sermon on the Mount, which begins with the Beatitudes, he spoke only to his disciples, those who had been chosen to understand and undertake the ministry of Jesus. In this context then, these words are addressed to the man and woman, the husband and wife, called and set apart for a different kind of life—marriage—that will reflect these qualities of the kingdom.

The Beatitudes describe the kind of person we are called to be, the person who responds to the gift of the

Gospel by living a life of choice, not of chance. That person knows, at heart, the call of God to be set apart not for a life of isolation, but for a life to be lived with and for others.

These words describe saints, the special vessels of God's grace in every generation, and it is not surprising that this text is also used on All Saints' Day. So these words might describe any one of us, for the saint is not so much a person of perfection as of refraction and reflection. The saint responds to the life given by God with the willingness to be a vessel, a channel, an instrument of God's grace.

No better definition of a saint was ever offered than that given by the ten year old girl, who was asked the question, "What is a saint?" She had not the slightest idea, but she did remember that as she sat in church, allowing her thoughts to drift far, far away, she would look to her right and to her left at the brilliant colored windows, which cast beautiful rays of red and green and blue and violet light across her. In those windows were figures of radiant men and women of another time and place. And so the little girl answered, "A saint is a person who lets in the light."

The call of marriage is the call to sainthood, the call to love of neighbor. The world created in marriage is the one centered in the love of God and expressed in the life and work of these two persons. Everything radiates outward from the marriage, the center for these two people, and in this center God dwells.

*   *   *

. . . He watched her move among the poor, the downtrodden, the outcast. She was a natural, a vessel of the love of God that she offered to others with authority and grace, tenderness and toughness, just as he imagined Jesus had done. She was more than a gift, she was the very presence of God in his midst. Her presence was strength and comfort; he always remembered then that to whom much is given, even more will be required. Yet she was unaware of what she did, although without a doubt she knew who made it all possible. Long ago she had been told that the central question was, "Who shall separate us from the love of Christ?" And the answer was no one, no thing, nothing at all. The love of Christ was as integral to her as their love one for another. The two were inextricably bound.

*   *   *

"You are the salt of the earth; but if salt has lost its taste, how can its saltness be restored? It is no longer good for anything except to be thrown out and trodden under foot by men.

You are the light of the world. A city set upon a hill cannot be hid. Nor do men light a lamp and put it under a bushel, but on a stand, and it gives light to all in the house. Let your light so shine before men, that they may see your good works and give glory to your father who is in heaven."

- MATTHEW 5: 13-16

On the path to full maturity, if we are ever to make it, each of us faces a decision about marriage and a decision about vocation. If we are to be whole people, the two decisions are related; each of us is called, through the gift of marriage, to live in the world with and for others. The call is not reserved for a chosen few. It may well be that many are called and few chosen, but this is only another way of saying that everyone is called but only a few respond. To fail to respond is to live only a portion of the life which has been made available to each of us.

To follow a call to a chosen work makes us whole, and it is this wholeness which is offered and shared in marriage. Without the call and the work we have less to offer, and so the marriage is less, sustained by less. But given the call and the work, then the marriage not only receives but embraces and nourishes and then responds. The call and the work become more, for this is part of the marriage. Vocation must be an individual, independent concern and decision, to be sure, but in marriage it becomes the very stuff of interdependence.

The oft-stated claim, "I did not marry a doctor (lawyer, priest, teacher, naval officer, civil engineer), I married a person," is fallacious. Granted that in the best of all worlds none of us is defined by the work we do, nevertheless, if the work is in response to a call, then that work becomes an extension and expression of the self. It is quite clearly a part of the marriage; we may not have named that job, but we did marry the person who held it or came to hold it. The vocation is very much a part of the person and so very much a part of the marriage.

*   *   *

. . . The young college teacher had done her graduate work in the sociology of the family, through time, in her own county, and she was deeply caught up in the field and its literature. Yet she strongly resisted any significant personal interest in her work, and it remained merely "statistics" for her or, at times, even "psychohistory," a discredited field amongst those she admired.

Until the time came for her to assume a position at another university, she had kept from fellow teachers and her students the information that she despised any kind of family affair—baptism, marriage, burial. "I belong to no one," she stated with conviction. The only child of older, uneducated parents, the teacher sought new status through education and chose the history and development of the family as her field. She was partner to a deliberately childless marriage with a professional man, not an academic, whose work was different in every way, from hers. How long could marriage embrace such discontinuity? As it turned out, three years.

*   *   *

If marriage and vocation are to reinforce one another, then there must be a common vision, a common purpose and goal in which each partner participates, even though they each walk a separate road. Vocation is an individual matter, but still one that both members of a marriage share—equally and in both directions. Each is called. As both are called, so each must share with the other a common calling to which they respond in vocation and marriage.

Actor Jack Lemmon and I grew up in the same town, attended neighboring schools, and graduated, a decade apart, from the same college. Though I didn't know him, he has always held a certain fascination for me. His film, "Mass Appeal" drew us to a holiday showing. Lemmon appeared as an aging but charming and glib Roman Catholic priest, who persevered in a difficult situation. The film subtly but clearly stated that the priest, his vocation, the Church and the Gospel of Christ were all a sham—hollow and useless.

Although we left the film in good moods, it had not been over for ten minutes when, for no apparent reason at all, we began a fight. The fight quickly escalated to become a battle, and then a deep and wrenching conflict. It was many hours, two days, before what had taken place became clear. The challenge to my calling as a priest was received and interpreted by both of us as a threat to everything that mattered, which meant, above all, our marriage.

When we finally came to some kind of peace, we were told that our eldest daughter was to be married.

"Every one then who hears these words of mine and does them will be like a wise man who built his house upon the rock; and the rain fell and the floods came, and the winds blew, and beat upon that house, but it did not fall, because it had been founded on the rock. And every one who hears these words of mine and does not do them will be like a foolish man who built his house upon the sand; and the rains fell, and the floods came, and the winds blew and beat against that house, and it fell; and great was the fall of it."

- MATTHEW 7: 24-29

"An affair wants to leak," wrote John Updike.

Two realities of human relationship are beyond
question.   First, we have an innate ability to shield
ourselves from being really known. Second, we love to
meddle in other people's business for nefarious reasons.
Newspapers, investigative reporters, and private
detectives, among others, derive their livelihood from
these realities.

If this is the case, then it can only be true that if Mr.
Smith is sneaking out with Mrs. Jones and the world
knows it, that is exactly their intention. "An affair wants
to leak." Why is the clandestine telephone message first
left on the telephone machine, "by mistake," and then
described in detail at lunch for the benefit of friends of
the wronged spouse the very next day? The cases are
legion.

What happens in relationship between the sexes is
what one wants to happen. The so-called overpowering
forces of romantic attraction that sometimes sweep
down and destroy a marriage are merely rationalization.
It has been said that Americans carry their brains in
their loins, which is but another way of stating the
obvious—we do what we want to do. Should we want
to have an affair, then, it can not be a secret; it is intended. Part of that intention is the end of the marriage.

A marriage is not a chancy undertaking. It is built
and it grows and develops or shrivels and dies in
accordance with very simple guidelines. There are no
surprises. If one fails to invest one's self and one's time
and energy in the marriage, it will deteriorate. If one is
drawn into or seeks intimate companionship with other
people, the marriage will fail. The events of a human
life bound in the covenant of marriage must be revealed
within that marriage. When they are not, then the

foundation and the building materials are full of cracks
and rot and open air, and the creation will crumble.

*   *   *

. . . They had married right after his graduation from the
state university. She didn't stay around to finish; she
liked school, but what was the point? In this, as in so
many things, they were simply doing what was expected
of them; they had known each other for years, so had
their parents. It never occurred to them to wait, to
explore life further; their parents hadn't, and why
should they? After all, it was important to get married
and not to be alone anymore, start a family.

He went into his father's business. She found a part-
time job, which gave her time to see her mother and her
sister almost every day. She got pregnant once, twice,
three times in succession. One child followed right on
the next, that wasn't the plan, but she was too tired and
dazed to plan. Her mother and sister helped her while
he worked for his father, and soon each was spending
more and more time with their own families and less
and less with each other.

As the children grew in age, however, there was
more and more time for fishing, encouraged by the
strong interest of their mutual friends, a neighboring
couple of similar ages and tastes. In time it was virtually
every weekend that the four of them were off together.
Fishing had become a passion.

As it turned out, however, fishing was not her
passion at all. At the end of a year she announced that
she was leaving to marry the other man, her fishing
companion. He, she had discovered, had time and in-

terest, and yes, passion, to share with her. Of course, what he really shared with her was himself. Fishing was a symbol, the medium through which each could be, one to the other, who they really were. They could be, one to the other, who they had not been in the bond of their former marriages. Something had been held back, something essential. This they opened one to another and were able to appear, each to the other, fully, honest, naked, without shame—and no longer willing to be alone.

They who once dreamed themselves Tristan-Isold
walk now invulnerable to dream, their sorrow spent,
their joy, a fallen star enshrined and cold.
But you and I, my dear, began with stone
armored upon our hearts defiantly.
The winds and weathers of our years have blown
our defences down and set us free.
Let us walk forth now on our ripened fields
and pluck what fruits of love the season yields.

"As the Father has loved me, so have I loved you; abide in my love. If you keep my commandments, you will abide in my love, just as I have kept my Father's commandments and abide in his love. These things I have spoken to you, that my joy may be in you, and that your joy may be full."

This is my commandment, that you love one another as I have loved you.

- JOHN 15: 9-12

Jesus' preaching to his disciples about love—his command that they love one another, as he has loved them—is the climax of the gospel readings for a marriage. With these words Jesus describes a quality of life and personal interaction that is to define both his body, the Church, and this marriage. The new commandment is for this man and this woman; it defines the condition which they are entering. The new commandment speaks to them about their love, one for another, their love for their neighbor, and all those who live with them in this world made by God and redeemed by Christ. "This is my commandment, that you love one another, as I have loved you."

The particular power of the commandment is he who speaks it. The same words spoken by Joe or Mary or our next door neighbor, would be different. As he has loved us, so it is possible for us to love one another. And so, within the gift of marriage, it is possible for us to be Christ one to another as in no other relationship which we shall ever know this side of heaven.

*   *   *

. . . They had been married for sixty-two years and one day. Both of them knew that it would happen sooner or later, that one would be taken and the other left. But they tried not to think about that. What good did it do? And if, for all these years, they had been so bound together, not two but one, then why should this not always be so? Neither one of them could really remember the time when they had not lived together as one.

It happened early one morning, eight o'clock of a Tuesday. He felt an unaccustomed pain in his left arm, which became worse and worse and then moved up, grasping his entire chest like a vise. He kept it from her for some time, but then, pale, as he tried to rise from the breakfast table, he fell. She rushed to his side. He was breathing heavily, gasping. She called the town's ambulance and then her daughter, who lived only around the corner. The daughter arrived first, and they both huddled over the panting figure, still trying to rest on the floor.

The EMTs arrived.   Both women insisted they wanted to ride with him in the ambulance.   "Just a moment, just a moment. I must go and get my things." And the wife of sixty-two years rushed upstairs.

Minutes later the daughter heard her fall, and rushed up the stairs, calling after her to the EMTs to follow.

He died in the ambulance before they could reach the hospital. She was dead by the time they had wheeled her into the Emergency Room.

After sixty-two years and one day, only ten minutes had separated their certified moments of death, celebrating and blessing, even at the end, the things which remain.

AMONG THE SWIFT AND VARIED CHANGES OF THE WORLD

THE MARRIAGE

No time now to stop and consider the consequences. If there were, surely one would freeze and the other flee. Instead, man and woman, two witnesses, and priest move forward, away from the others. They may move a few feet or as many as a hundred, but the significance is the same. This is their business, theirs alone. The rest of us watch and wait. As we do, nothing magical changes this man and this woman in the twinkling of an eye, yet everything changes.

In the Name of God,

The concept of name in the biblical tradition is extremely powerful. The use of name, invoked here, is serious business. The Bible understands the use of name to signal complete and total knowledge, real understanding, of all that other person is, was, and would be. Whenever the Bible cites a name or gives a name, that name means something, states a specific quality, calls forth a certain kind of person. And so when in the Bible a person of great significance undergoes a complete change of character (Jacob, Saul), then the name of that person is changed (Israel, Paul).

That can never be the case with God. The names for God are many throughout the Old and New Testaments; each is a close approximation to the real thing, but God's total, actual name is never mentioned. Who could possibly call God by name? No one, for no one knows God. Any attempt we make is merely an approximation.

So at the moment of the marriage we do not call upon God by name, but the presence of God is invoked. God, whom we can not completely know, understand or appreciate, is here with us in name. God is present and active, here and now, in the midst of this man and woman. They are the very centerpiece of God's new creation.

*   *   *

. . . The room was crowded with people whom we had never met. The hosts, whom we knew only slightly, moved towards us, threading their way slowly through their guests. The light was dim, created largely by candles, firelight, and blinking lights on two large Norfolk pines, standing in opposite corners and decorated as Christmas trees. Finally, they reached us, and we greeted one another awkwardly, each speaking the name of the other only with the greatest of difficulty. It was not an easy situation, and for a moment we wondered if we should have come at all.

The woman went about her business with others; her husband, grasping each of us by an elbow, guided us across the room and introduced us to an "old friend," whose name we never caught. Nevertheless, we talked for several minutes until joined by old friends of his and introductions were in order. The use of names became difficult, clumsy, impossible; all conversation ended;

each person drifted off in a different direction. The sudden realization that names were absent ended even half-hearted attempts at communication.

She and I moved off in different directions, but not before I caught one phrase, cast over her shoulder, as she moved away, "I saw Sally."   Sally was the single person present whose name we knew and had a name for us.

Minutes later I found them together on a couch, talking in a quiet corner. Sally greeted me, easily, by name. We were new in town, but had enjoyed a previous long and comfortable time together. We knew her. Conversation flowed, mostly concerning family members, hers and ours, their names.

I, N.(ame), take you, N.(ame),

With what name are we to be married? What name should be used? Why, the given name, of course. But given by whom and for what purpose? Certainly not the surname, the family name, the name that is added on. Then it must be our first name, our Christian name, for it is with this name that we are baptized into Christ, his life, death and resurrection. It is the name by which we are known as Christians and known to Christ.

Yet names change over time. A baby is known by names of intimacy and endearment that are different again from the Christian name. The mother of the child may call her baby by a private name, unknown to any others, different from the name the father, or the brothers and sisters use. As the child grows and ventures into different situations and circumstances, forming friendships, names change and evolve. From the moment of birth, well beyond middle age, any single human being may have a dozen names. Over time, as we encounter friends we used to know, we are called by names we have not heard in years. Some special few know the name of "back then," the name of childhood, the special identity of a given moment.

The name which will be used on the occasion of a marriage will be a name known and recognized by all those present; however, its use signals unique knowledge. Two people have been brought to this point through the sharing of unusual intimacy. Now they stand at the threshold of a lifetime of knowing one another and use this name at the very beginning.

*   *   *

. . . Each Tuesday morning she and a small group of like-minded United Church Women visited the male geriatric ward in the Maryland State Mental Institution. For three hours once a week they would visit, play cards, read aloud, help with letter writing, whatever seemed most useful and needed at that time.

One particular man caught Aunt Eleanor's attention. He was totally unreachable, apparently a hopeless and incurable catatonic, who sat hunched in the corner, head down, body turned away from the rest of the room. Yet each Tuesday Aunt Eleanor went and spoke to him, often sat down and spent extra time. There was never any response, none at all. Still she persisted, each Tuesday, week after week after week.

In time, their visits became so frequent that if Mr. Gordon had heard all Aunt Eleanor had said to him, and she believed that he both heard and understood it all, then he knew a good deal about her. She, on the other hand knew nothing of him first-hand, although she had received permission to read the open parts of his file and had spoken at length to all the nurses and ward attendents.

It was the Tuesday before Christmas, when she stopped on her weekly rounds in his corner. "Why, good morning, Mr. Gordon. A very Merry Christmas to you." Mr. Gordon turned his head and looked Aunt Eleanor full in the face. "Good morning to you, Miss Richardson, and a very Merry Christmas to you."

It had been the very first time she had called him by name. The name created his response.

to be my wife,
to be my husband,

Each is called to be a new creation. This named and unique person is to be created anew as a wife, a husband. To be wife or husband to this particular and special other person is to stand in a relationship unlike any other we may have. We may be friend, confidante, mother, father, sister, brother, counselor, confessor, lover, but none of these comes close to being wife or husband. To be wife or husband is to be part of the other in the wholeness of one flesh.

We do not become married unless we are willing to explore this then unknown mystery, the identity of husband or wife, a dimension not to be fully fathomed even in a life-long marriage. The vows are undertaken with a long look forward and the readiness to undertake the mystery of becoming wife and husband.

to have . . .

Of the four verbs which embody the sacrament of marriage, this is the first. It is a remnant from a previous age when the husband quite literally possessed his wife. Virtually all other traces of this understanding of marriage have been removed, but this one has come to apply equally to husband and wife; it symbolizes the reality of mutual possession. Each person in marriage possesses the other. When this is absent, then the marriage will fail.

*   *   *

. . . The failure of their marriage was predictable, like so many others. Their interests were different, even opposed, while repeated miscarriages symbolized their inability to create or meet in any way. Each was strong, able, passionate, devoted to what was "important," but the marriage itself was never realized as central. So it dwindled and died, not merely in their inability to procreate, but even to encounter one another. Both had affairs, never discussed, but each knew.

When she began to drink heavily, it was just one more thing, a problem to be avoided. Even as the drinking became worse and worse, no one saw it was her misdirected way of telling him and the world that they did not belong to one another. No one, especially not her husband, could "have" her, and so she dissolved what was left of her life in gin. Towards the end she developed the habit of wandering off, when intoxicated, for a walk through the woods. There was no moon the night she decided to walk to the pond for a swim. The state police found her body the next morning.

The marriage was over, a marriage which had never been. Neither was ever willing to own or be owned.

to hold . . .

The verb, *to have* may be more symbolic than real, while *to hold* is more real than symbolic. If the marriage is not a matter of daily holding, then there will be no marriage.

Daily holding. Daily like bread and time and laughter. It is holding in the sense that each belongs to the other, that each owns the other, past, present and future. It is the physical act of touch and grasp and hug.

*   *   *

. . . During a particularly stressful period in their lives, she developed an ominous, lingering ache in her side. She said nothing about it to him until it had become severe, daily, hourly. When finally she spoke, he responded with panic and helped immediately with all the necessary arrangements to see the doctor who cared for them in every circumstance. She, however, delayed and resisted, mindful of the more than two packs of cigarettes she smoked every day and her good friend only last month dead from cancer of the lungs. The ache continued, if anything worse than before. Finally she went to the doctor, but he could report nothing and refused to offer a conclusion until the x-ray had been returned and read.

Twenty four hours passsed. The doctor called at work. The x-rays were clear. She must have pulled a muscle.

Elated, she telephoned her husband and arranged to meet at a restaurant to celebrate the good news. It was as though many years had been returned to them, years that she feared had been lost. Later, as they climbed into bed, and shifted around, looking for a comfortable position, he reached out, as he always did, especially when life was tense and difficult. He put his arms around her and pulled her toward him with affection and determination. She cried out in pain. "That's the spot!" In an instant they both understood the cause of her recent injury and their anxiety. He held her. Suddenly, the past was swallowed up in laughter.

from this day forward,

Marriage is life-long. Any other expectation is not of marriage but some other form of contractual agreement. The reason for this is crystal clear.

Human beings conform to expectations. What they achieve is precisely what they expect to achieve, or what others expect for them. Each of us lives within the tension of a very delicate balance created by our own expectations and the expectations held for us.

*   *   *

. . . His father was taciturn, so when he offered advice, the boy always remembered it. Each September, the start of the new school year, his father repeated the same speech to him. "The first eight weeks are the most important. The first eight weeks, everything which contributes to that first set of grades, is crucial. The impression you create and the reputation you gain for yourself will never be fully changed after that. Work as hard and as well as you can." And it turned out to be true, again and again, especially if the academic environment were new. Once an expectation was created, you lived within it, and in turn, it formed you, just as you had formed it.

*   *   *

By and large people conform to the expectations set for them. This insight is reflected in the marriage liturgy, which insists that marriage is *only* undertaken and understood as a life-long commitment. Under any other conditions marriage will be something far less.

The high number of marriages ending in divorce is caused largely by two factors. The first is teen-age marriage. Eliminate from the divorce statistics all those marriages entered into during the teens, and the number of divorces will drop markedly. A second, more subtle factor, is the divorce statistics themselves. Consciously or unconsciously, each and every person who enters into a marriage contract is very well aware of the fact that only fifty percent of all marriages undertaken in the United States today survive. It is the expectation, therefore, that half of all marriages will not be "from this day forward . . . until we are parted by death." Many people determine that they will be among the failures, and as a result their marriages do fail.

There is no real reason this should be the case. Few of us believe that we shall be among the more than 40% of the population who suffer from cancer, nor the 12% who will become alcoholic. Quite the contrary, we assume that we shall escape these killers. Fifty thousand persons will die each year in automobile accidents, but it does not occur to us that we might be struck by a drunken driver when we venture out on the road. Yet those being married too often assume that their marriage will not succeed, simply because they know that one in two marriages fail. The statistics proclaim that marriage is a risky business, and many assume that this will be true for them, not that they will be in the other, more successful half!

Long ago, Christians standing within the Catholic tradition understood this in simpler form. The contract which each of us undertakes is lifelong, until we are parted by death. It does not last merely until either one or the other thinks better of the idea, and it is not until another option is offered. The certainty of life-long union is clear and absolutely essential.

*   *   *

. . . Their children were still quite small, perhaps twelve and ten and six, when they spent several days driving to Maine to take the eldest to summer camp. It was the first time any of the younger children had been away for so long a period of time, and the parents decided to make an outing of the event and spend the weekend at a comfortable country inn.

When they came back Saturday afternoon after a day of exploring, it was clear that the inn had been the scene of a wedding reception. Floral decorations were everywhere, dishes still being rushed to the kitchen, rice covered all of the floors and carpets. More unusual still was the sight of many discarded copies of the marriage contract littering all the public rooms of the inn.

At dinner, the ten-year-old gathered sufficient copies of the contract for each of them to read. All sat about the table, after ordering dinner, and studied the contract. There were several provisions, signed and attested to by the two partners. These itemized the amount of time which husband and wife would spend with the other, as well as the amount of financial compensation which the wife would receive for the pain of childbirth. The final condition was that this contract would be subject to review and renewal at each third and fifth anniversary.

After the document was read and considered, the ten-year-old asked for opinions. Before any were offered, however, she could not resist giving her conclusion. "They won't be married in three years."

Exactly three years later, returning to the same inn to attend and participate in a wedding, the innkeeper was asked if he knew anything of the couple who had staged the elaborate ceremony there three years ago. "Yes, I remember them very well," he said." Such an idealistic couple. Sad, very sad. They never even celebrated their first anniversary."

*   *   *

Two realities, both opposites, seem to be true of those who seek counsel at the time of marital trouble.

The first insight I heard years ago from a professional counselor and Episcopal priest in Washington, who maintained that those who came to him for help in a troubled marriage sought only one thing: the salvation of the marriage. They sought out this counselor precisely because he was a priest commited to the life-long survival of the marriage. In his presence they knew they could rant and rave and rail about the other and about the prison to which they had been consigned in the marriage bond, but the counselor, in the end, would surely advise them that the marriage could survive.

The second reality is far more frequent. Counselors involved in helping those with troubled marriages frequently report discouragement with their work *if* the healing they seek to promote is the salvation of the marriage. Most frequently the couple involved will not seek counsel until they both believe that the marriage

has already ended; however, if it is to be dissolved, a
higher authority must authorize the dissolution. They
go to the marriage counselor and present their case and
ask for a blessing. Their intention is not to work to heal
the union, only to ask the counselor to agree with the
decision they have made.

Deep down inside each person there remains the
sense that no individual has the right to end a marriage.
The contract is for life, as the vow makes clear. But
sometimes the pain is too great, and there is the wish to
be released from the daily and living sense of failure.

*   *   *

. . . The elderly woman being interviewed on national
televsion was grand, eloquent, and much admired. Her
life-long marriage of more than fifty years had been
ended in the past year by her husband's death. "Come
now, " the interlocutor chided. "There must have been
some days, several perhaps, when you really wanted to
divorce your husband." The response was quick and
passionate and fiery. "Murder, yes! Divorce, never!"

*   *   *

Such wisdom understands the fact that marriage,
true and life-long marriage, will know moments of
bitter hate and pain, perhaps distrust. Both spouses
must know, even in moments of closest intimacy and
joy, that ahead lie times of temptation and agony, and at
such times, only one thing will remain: their vow.

The marriage sealed with the words, "until we are
parted by death" is a marriage conceived and continued
in the context of the Christian gospel. The symbol of

that gospel is a cross, a cross of suffering and death and a cross of passion. The promise of that passion is that as we pass with Christ through suffering and death, so too we shall be raised with him to new life. This is not a once-in-a-lifetime experience. The gospel and the sacrament of marriage proclaim that the experience of suffering and death will happen again and again, and when it does, if we dodge or back away or run to some kind of false refuge, there will be no new life. We know all too well that the inevitable valley of death, through which we shall pass more than once, is a place of many, bitter tears, and the tears are our own. But these very same tears, these tears of pain and torment, are the only tears that will ever become tears of joy and thanksgiving. They are essential to our life in Christ.

Moments of death and transition within a marriage will occur almost at predictable intervals. The comedy "The Seven Year Itch," popular in a previous Broadway generation, was intended to be humorous; its subject is not. Pain, strife and sorrow will occur at approximately seven and fifteeen and twenty one and thirty and more years of marriage, predictable turning points that mark growth and new opportunity. Failure to move through such transitions into the new life that lies on the other side will produce death and dissolution. The necessity for change does not mean that whatever went before was useless, only that the willingness to move beyond was absent. Men and women who do not evolve and grow, atrophy and die, literally or figuratively. A marriage is no different.

*   *   *

. . . The marriage was three years old. Something had been brewing for days, and it erupted following dinner on a Tuesday night. Neither of them could remember how it all started. Something small, something stupid, and before either knew what had happened he could be clearly heard across the street calling her "Bitch!" and worse, and she was screaming unintelligible profanities. The Quimper sugar bowl hit the wall and shattered; the kitchen table overturned with a crash; finally, in exhaustion, each withdrew. She sat, alone, up on the landing on the stairs. He lay, face down, in the middle of the living room. Neither could see or hear the other. They remained that way for hours.

It was after the clock struck midnight that he finally raised his head and asked, "What are you doing?" No answer. He spoke again. Still no answer, and an even longer pause. After fifteen minutes, she said, "I'm making a list. I'm making a list of all the things about you which I can't stand."

"Oh," he replied. "I made mine two weeks ago. It never occurred to me that you might make one too."

Another pause. Then she rose and descended the stairs ever so slowly and entered the living room and lay down beside him.

* * *

. . . The elderly French couple lived in the United States most of their married lives and devoted themselves to one another and the culture of their adopted city. After his wife died, he was never the same again, although his life continued for several years, alone, built about his memories of her. Shortly before his own death, he told an old friend of the poem he had written for his wife on their last anniversary together, which began, "*Ce matin pour notre anniversaire.*" To celebrate the anniversary, he had tried to give his wife two rose-buds, one for each of them. She refused them, because one would die, leaving the other alone.

And so he wrote for her and repeated to his friend on that day from memory. "*Alors je ne t'en ai donné qu'une. C'est mieux comme cela. Toi et moi, nous sommes une seule chose. Pas deux, une seule. Complétement unis et ensemble pour l'Éternité. C'est mieux comme cela.*"

"So I gave you one. It is better this way. You and I, we are only one thing. Not two, but one. Completely at one, together for eternity. It is better this way."

for better for worse . . .

Frequently quoted, usually only in jest, these four words are the focus of little real attention, yet they come close to the very essence of marriage. It is understandable why they are avoided. As two people look forward to the hoped-for lifetime of love and fulfillment, they hardly wish to anticipate that the life they face together is the occasion for good times mixed with bad. All will not be sweetness and light. There will be hard and bitter and painful times, stress both from within and without the marriage. And so standing here, looking to the horizon of all the man and woman promise one another, they also assert that marriage bonds them "for better for worse."

This is a vital and unusual concept. Marriage is not undertaken because times will always be good. Marriage is undertaken precisely because they will not always be good. Whenever a test is faced, no matter what that test may be, it is never the reason to push the eject button, to try to escape.   The time of the test is the time to realize why marriage has been created.

*   *   *

. . . Three men went on a cruise down the coast of Maine on a beautiful June weekend. The northwest wind was unusually brisk. No one ever knew how it happened, but they never returned. After a week, there was a memorial service, and the next day the Coast Guard found first one body and then the others. Time passed. It did not seem it could get any worse. It didn't.

None of it should have happened. The whole event was cruel and senseless, especially for the young widow, who, having survived her husband's marine duty in Vietnam, was now joined with him in raising a young family and becoming established in important work as leaders in a new community. If there could be any good in the midst of her horror, it was the love and support of friends who offered to help provide her new life.

One effort was her friends' introduction to a new friend. The meeting was carefully planned to be casual, and it started a whirlwind courtship, a proposal after six weeks, and then marriage into her town and home, where it was difficult for her to welcome him so suddenly, so soon. All soon learned that he had come to stay, for better for worse.

This marriage, like every other, was both better and worse. There was joy and passion and laughter, only then the children were difficult and combative. Once they accepted their new father, there was loss—death, first one parent, then another. Wife and husband knew what others learn only with time. Death is inevitable, essential to life and marriage. Bitter and painful, death is partner to this and every marriage.

*   *   *

There is a text from the New Testament that speaks of a difficult and haunting reality which pervades the deepest places of our lives. "Truly, truly, I say to you, unless a grain of wheat falls into the earth and dies, it remains alone; but if it dies, it bears much fruit." (John 12: 24). We are blocked from that perception by our culture, which constantly proclaims reality is only found in getting and saving and consuming. The constant hope is that our fulfillment lies just around the corner —it is the next opportunity, the next challenge, the next vacation, the next thrill. Occasionally, we realize that each "next" leads nowhere, although usually by that time it is too late. The death which has arrived is not even a real death. It is the death of a child's over-used new toy winding down for the last time on Christmas night. The thrill has been wasted and is now just as flat as the stale taste of too much ribbon candy.

*   *   *

. . . For more than twenty-five of their thirty-four years of married life it *had* all been better—better and better. Their love was strong, their intellectual companionship deep, their sexual relationship constantly moving to greater depths of intimacy. Brought together in college, the basis of their marriage lay in the professional success each earned and shared, as well as the birth of two bright and beautiful children, first a boy and then a girl. He created his own business in a part of the country new to

both of them.   They became established, known, re-
spected, and the children grew and thrived.

Then something happened. It all changed. The son
was killed in an airplane accident. The daughter, whose
entire life had been wrapped up in her family, became
deeply depressed. Nothing was the same; it went from
bad to worse. He became morose, detached and distant.
And why not? The Board of Directors of the company
which had prospered through his brilliance and hard
work, *his* company, called for his resignation. At sixty,
life seemed over. Everything was gone.

Yet the marriage remained, for better for worse.
Rooted in God and steeped in prayer, it was a marriage
full of their own love and the love which had infused
their vow. Neither one could fully understand it, but
they knew it to be present, as they clung to each other,
and repeated the old words. The words were not hollow.
They were real, and again they took root. It could not get
any worse. It was better. Better and better.

for richer for poorer . . .

If too little attention is focused on "for better for
worse," then the words "for richer for poorer" receive
too much—and attention of the wrong kind. Our
culture's reduction of every experience, every emotion,
everything to monetary value pervades each level of
society. That is how marriage is evaluated—by those
who observe it, by members of the family, by the couple
itself. We are encouraged to evaluate a prospective mate
as we might a purchase or a purveyor of goods and
services—what will it do for me, my appearance,
reputation and advancement, to be publicly and in-
timately associated with this person?   "Marrying for
money" may really seldom happen, but it is the most

frequently mentioned and easily identified form of this reality.

*   *   *

. . . It was one of the most terrifying and indelible memories of his late childhood. On a Sunday afternoon in mid-winter, he had retreated to his bedroom above the kitchen to finish his homework. His eldest sister had come home from college, and after the family dinner, she and her mother and father were in the kitchen finishing cleaning up after the mid-day meal. The clanking of pots and pans mixed with the muffled sound of their voices.

Suddenly, there was a silence. Then voices started up again, loud voices resounding from the kitchen and up the stairs to his room. He rose from his desk and moved into the upper hall to sit on the top stair. He sat there for half an hour.

His sister had told to her parents of her desire to marry her childhood sweetheart, recently home from overseas and back in state college. He had never been acceptable to the family, was not what the parents had in mind for their first born. Now they made their feelings loud and clear.

"He'll never earn more than ten thousand dollars! If that's what you want, go right ahead. But remember, you were warned. Oh, he's all right. A nice young man. But he can never support you. He'll never amount to anything. Do you have any idea what it will be like for you to exist on ten thousand dollars? Do you have any idea what I earn a year, what it takes to support this family in the humble way in which you have been raised? I can assure you it is somewhat more than a lousy ten thousand a year."

The sounds were not familiar, jarring in this house in which he had lived his entire life. Many times afterward he had wished he could remove the memory. The marriage took place, of course, the parents had assured that. So, too, the marriage failed, long after the parents, who made sure of this as well, had died. The young man in question became a millionaire.

*   *   *

"For richer for poorer." If we are ever tempted to believe that marriage is a commercial enterprise, remember that this is not the reason behind this vow. It is part of a series of extreme conditions—better, worse, rich, poor, sick, well—stating that marriage is undertaken and sustained for *all* conditions, no matter what they may be. Marriage is not a commercial enterprise; it is an act of worship.

Money is the symbol of power, a center for worship. Money symbolizes love and care and frustration; it is very often the excuse to leave unsaid many things, known and unknown, remembered and forgotten. Money demands a great deal of insight and the clear knowledge that there is no right or wrong way to handle it, despite all the advice. The management of money has to do with stewardship and reputation and image and the desire for immortality; it seldom has anything to do with money. Money has become a thing in and of itself, when it is actually only a symbol of the great end and real business of living. But to deal with the real purpose of life makes us all feel uncomfortable, so we talk instead of money and, too often, talk of nothing at all.

*   *   *

. . . They were stuffing the Thanksgiving turkey together. It was a happy occasion. Tomorrow, for the very first time, the members of both families would gather under their roof for the great feast. After thirteen years of marriage, they knew they were grown up. Only grown up people entertained more than twenty family members about a groaning board on the American family feast day.

The only problem was that this was not something they had ever done before—stuffed a Thanksgiving turkey together. Always they had been elsewhere on Thanksgiving, never at home. There were two big birds. It would have been simple enough for her to stuff one and he to stuff the other, but it was not to be. They decided to prepare one massive amount of stuffing, together, to be used for both turkeys. Only his mother had prepared stuffing in one way and her mother in another. The methods were completely different, and there was no way, no way at all, for them to be compatible.

The fight began at a high pitch and then escalated further. Two different families, their backgrounds, their past, their intrinsic worth were at once at issue. Somehow money very soon became the coin of intercourse and exchange in the conflict. Whose money had purchased the turkeys, provided for the stuffing and the rest of the meal? And if it was his money—or was it hers?—then what did that have to do with Thanksgiving and dinner and what was served and who sat where and why and when they were going to arrive?

The battle went round and round, without resolution. Somehow the turkeys did get stuffed and prepared for roasting. Before long it was not just money, but virtually every aspect of the marriage which was at stake. Why had they come to this point? Neither wanted it. Intense fatigue and the absence of sexual intimacy played its usual and destructive role. Nothing could help them. They came close to final and total dissolution. Only after each had hurt the other to the limit of ability, and all energy was gone, and they found each other in the bed that had bound them together through all these years, and at last there was release in sleep—only then were they able to stop and with reason and insight define the power and intensity of money, its use and place, in their marriage.

in sickness and in health . . .

Health speaks of wholeness, oneness, integration, well-being in its many forms. It is the very reason for marriage: two whole and healthy human beings are joined together to form a new, greater, healthy union. Health is the what and why and how of marriage.

Yet in the words of the vow, sickness comes first. Two people are married in sickness *and* in health. They are married not because they will always be whole, but because they will often be broken. They are married not because they will always be able to give to one another all each has to offer, but precisely because they will be unable to do so. They are married to bind together their brokenness, their sickness, and with it to create a whole marriage.

The husband of British mystery writer P. D. James returned from the Second World War mentally ill. Sometimes violent, he was constantly in and out of hospitals. She thought at first that his illness would be temporary, but then it became clear that he was unlikely ever to be well again, and she made the necessary changes to incorporate the illness into their lives, into their marriage.

She never considered divorce. "No. Never. Never. Never. I loved my husband. I took him for better or worse, richer or poorer, in sickness and in health. Divorce is very bad for children. He was a very good father; he loved the children very much; he loved me. I was never the sort of woman who could throw over her husband because he proved to be mentally or physically ill. It wasn't his fault."

To be sick means to be out of step, out of tune, in a state of dis-ease. So much of the time, I am out of touch and suffering. But to the moment and momentum of this suffering there comes another person, a person who offers that self to make me whole. From the realization that from my brokenness there can be a whole, that from my sickness there can be health, comes love. "To fall in love" means only that - to become whole, to become one with another.

to love and to cherish , until we are parted by death.

These are tender and difficult words, usually evoking tears from every witness at the marriage. Such a wonderful and impossible vow. It is the vow which encompasses everything else that takes place here and now.

To cherish is to hold dear. It is one of the ways of realizing worth, proclaiming that here is a pearl of great price, the center of my life and being, the object of my affections, far more important to me than anything else could be. We state publically before the altar of God that each has and holds the other—wholly—not just the best part, but all parts. It is popular in our age to believe that I enter into and experience marriage in every respect except one: I still reserve a part of my self for myself, alone, no one else may invade or know. That is me and me alone. It is not a part of marriage; it is out of the reach of my wife or husband.

Yet we need to be known, fully, through and through, and to be valued in spite of this. No part of me may hold back from this vow, if there is to be a vow binding us, now and always. Naked and alone we came into this world, and so we remain, save with one other and one other alone. That other is the one who cherishes and loves me, just as I am, all that I am, warts and welts, grace and glory, loves and cherishes me for the first and last time this side of the grave.

*   *   *

... My friend came late to the meeting. Everyone else sat waiting, for without him, there would be no meeting. And when he arrived, he walked haltingly to the seat in the center of the room. The rest of us waited for him to call the meeting to order.

He began to to speak slowly and with some difficulty of how and why he had been detained. He and an old friend were proceeding home together, at the hour of dusk, out of town and in heavy traffic along the boulevard by the river. Progress was slow, with much stopping and starting.

Just as the downtown traffic began to move again and his car gathered momentum, a jogger ran, without warning and without looking, directly across the heavy traffic, from right to left. He had almost made it across, when my friend's car hit him full on, at the lefthand, forward corner. The runner was thrown up upon the hood, passed over the top of the automobile and fell, with a heavy thud, behind them.

As if by a miracle, the car immediately to the rear was a metropolitan police cruiser. The policeman was the first on the scene and then a small crowd began to gather. From it emerged a nurse, just on her way home from the great hospital complex at the base of the river basin behind them. The nurse bent over the body, while the policeman summoned an ambulance by radio. There was nothing for anyone else to do.

Then, he said, as he told the story to the circle of faces, "An amazing thing happened." Some color came back to his face, his voice gathered strength.

"All of a sudden, from out of the small crowd that had gathered about from the stalled cars behind, I felt a hand slip into mine, my right hand, into my pocket. It came from behind, and it was connected to a person, a voice. In the midst of all this horror, she was there. I turned and as we hugged each other, I said, 'I knew it was you. You are always there. For forty years you've been there. No matter when, no matter what, we have been together.'"

He paused. There was much shuffling of feet and staring at the the rug and at other people's shoes throughout the room.

This is my solemn vow.

. . . He had been married once before, for twenty-five years to his childhood sweetheart. Towards the end, they had just grown apart one from another. Nothing really had happened. That was the problem; the marriage ended, without a sound. His two children were grown and on their own, and for a significant time he lived all alone, trying to center on his work and his friends. Then through a business associate he met a young woman, not yet thirty, fresh and spirited; he was young for fifty, and the two were remarkably suited to each other. It was a whirlwind courtship, and they decided to marry.

Their marriage was to take place in the house which they had planned and renovated themselves to become the center of their new life. Every detail of house and ceremony, all that lay ahead for them, was planned with the most loving care. It was a new adventure.

The service underway, she laughed out loud when he made his betrothal promise, "I will." It was as if she said to the world: "Did you hear what he just said? Why, he said that it was his intention to marry me!"

All went well until he began his marriage vows, slowly and laboriously. Each word, undertaken with the greatest solemnity, was spoken fully. Yet as he moved through his marriage vows to their powerful conclusion, he became more and more overcome with passion and emotion, and only with the greatest of difficulty was able to say, "until we are parted by death." Even then he anticipated the moment, a long way off, when the marriage would end, and he wanted to avoid it for as long as possible. Finally the words were spoken.

And then, in conclusion, it was his task to seal it all with the words, "This is my solemn vow." Emotion overwhelmed him as his line of vision, across the small room, his very own study, caught the eye of his daughter, only a few years younger than the woman he had just promised to marry. He could not speak; it seemed as if minutes passed. His chin quivered, his mouth opened and shut, and opened again. No words formed.

At long last it seemed best not to prolong the moment; the bride began her vow, "In the Name of God. . ." It was then, and only then, at the mention of the name of the deity, that his tongue was loosed. The words rushed forth like a torrent: "This is my solemn vow!"

THE RINGS

Bless, O Lord, these rings to be signs of the vows by which this man and this woman have bound themselves to each other; through Jesus Christ our Lord. Amen.

The place of the ring in this liturgy has changed through time. At first the ring was only worn by the woman, put upon her finger by the man to show that she was now his property. A woman had no rights, little identity, held no property, existed in fact only as a piece of property. She was brought to the church by her father, who bore her down the aisle and presented her by the hand to the priest, who in turn delivered her to the man. The man, having sworn his oath to her and received her oath in return, placed a ring upon her finger, as evidence of this transaction, legal and holy, which made her his.

In some parts of our culture the strong prejudice against men wearing any kind of jewelry finds its origin in the place of the wedding ring as a statement of possession; however, in Christian marriage both the man and the woman wear a ring as a sign of their vow, a statement to the world of all that marriage proclaims

and entails. The place and purpose of the rings has been
redeemed, elevated to a new level of meaning.

I give you this ring as a symbol of my vow,

The rings are given and received with these words.
Blessed as a "sign" by the celebrant, these rings point to
the fact of the vow. When the rings are given and received, however, there is something more. The ring is
also a symbol, more powerful than a mere sign. Not
only does a symbol point to the reality it symbolizes, it is
part of it. Once placed upon the finger, the ring *is* the
vow. It embodies that vow, it bears and maintains it.

*   *   *

. . . The wedding rings they wore had been engraved
with four verbs: "have, hold, love cherish." The vow
and rings were a unity. The vows could no longer be
read, what with wear and time; they had been ground
into the gold and were part of it.

Aware that these rings were as much a part of the
essential person as the fingers that wore them, he would
often find himself staring at the naked ring finger of another person, someone who had once been married and
had cast off the marriage, the vow and the ring, in one
sweeping and complete motion. He would stare in order
to try and find the indelible impression the ring must
have left behind. When he found none, he wondered if
there had ever really been a marriage, or had it all been
merely a convenience?

and with all that I am, and all that I have, I honor you,

The words echo an older, more poetic statement,
now long discarded, "With my body I thee worship and

with all my worldly goods I thee endow." It is vital and emphatic; it has power. The entire being and identity of the giver, complete with all worldly goods are brought, symbolically, to this union and offered in honor to the other. It is an act of worship, one that does not reserve any corners, small or large, from the reality of marriage.

For the marriage vow is never merely a subjective state, but a dramatic, intentional reality. It is proclaimed first of all in the quality of the married life that this man and this woman create. The vow is enacted in the giving and receiving of rings, which are worn upon hands that express the whole person.

*   *   *

. . . Throughout childhood he could remember his father saying, again and again: "If you want to know who another person really is, look first to the hands. Clues will be found there in great abundance, more even than in the eyes. Are the nails bitten, hang nails pulled? What care and cleanliness are revealed? And what do you learn from shape? But there is more. Those hands are the extension of that person's life and livelihood. They are the intimate of that being, and with them, that person 'manipulates'—expresses the self—in the world. Look to the hands to find the person."

in the Name of the Father, and of the Son, and of the Holy Spirit.

. . . As they approached the twenty-fifth anniversary of their vows, they gathered together wedding bands from parents and grandparents, aunts and uncles. They collected all the old family gold that had been worn as the symbol of the vows which had bound together their

forebears and relations. These rings the local jeweler
cast into five rings. Three would be worn by their children as the symbol of the love which had created them.
Two would be cast into wedding bands, initialed and in-
scribed, to be placed on each others hands during the renewal of their vows at the celebration of their
anniversary.

And so it was that new rings were made from old
gold and worn to symbolize thanksgiving for the twenty-
five years now passed and anticipation of all the years
which lay ahead.

*Now that N. and N. have given themselves to each
other by solemn vows, with the joining of hands and
the giving and receiving of rings, I pronounce that they
are husband and wife, in the name of the Father, and of
the Son, and of the Holy Spirit.*

*Those whom God hath joined together let no one put
asunder.*

The vows are sealed with Jesus' strongest statement
regarding marriage. This proclamation of union, drawn
from the ancient passage from Genesis, brings home the
image of the whole person, first created by God from the
two selves of human nature, long ago separated, now
restored to complete wholeness. No one, for any purpose whatsoever, should stand between those "whom
God hath joined together," this man and this woman,
now united as a new creation.

The words are both theological and practical— immediate, for right now, but also for some unknown future moment and challenge. The words are brief and
clear and to the point and deeply serious. The marriage
conceived and undertaken in the name of Jesus will be

lived under this seal: joined by God, to be separated by
no one.

*   *   *

. . . The telephone call was unexpected and came from a
great distance. The news was urgent. The father of the
family, beloved by all, lay dying. There was no question.
Forty-eight hours. No more. You must come. He has
asked for you.

Twenty-four hours later the two men were alone
together. The older man had been his mentor and
friend. Taciturn, yet now powerfully articulate, his concern was with essentials.

"Our marriage has been extraordinary. Never have
we backed away from the challenges, always we have
stood together. Now we are to be parted. No, no, no.
Don't try to dissuade me. I am ready, really I am. Curious, I admit, but not afraid. The Lord has been more
than my shepherd. He has been guardian, guide and
friend. You and I have talked often of prayer; you know
what I mean.

"Only one thing matters now. The vows we made
were 'until death do us part.' That's not fair, and I refuse to accept it. It was the Lord himself who proclaimed: 'Those whom God has joined together let no
one put asunder.' Isn't that true? Don't let him separate
us. Not now. We are closer, dearer, more in love than
ever before. You know what we have been through together. I've almost died six times, and now I will. But
tell me that we shall never be parted."

There was a long silence. What could the younger
man say? These were the words which, if he could say

them at all, would carry the older man into everlasting life. At long last, he said this.

"Sam, nothing at all will ever separate you from the love of Christ. That is the love which has bound you together in this world. That is the love which will bind you together forever."

A NEW CREATION

Now they are a new creation. The very first words that husband and wife speak together are the words of The Lord's Prayer, the words upon which the marriage stands and lives and grows. The Lord's Prayer is a rule of life, a way of life, for those called to live together in marriage.

*   *   *

. . . There are moments in our lives, rare to be sure, when we know with clarity and assurance all we need to know. Questions do not exist, only answers. He remembered reading that Mircea Eliade created a word to describe just such a moment, "hierophany," which means "the sacred shows itself." Such moments are not predictable; they come and they go as they will, quite beyond our control. They happen while waking or sleeping, lost in a crowd or at peace in a meadow. This one happened while he was asleep.

As the dark turned to dawn, a time for prayer and reverie, he had a vision, a dream, and in the dream a figure appeared. It was a woman. Without waiting for her to speak, he asked, "What is the rule of life?" and she answered, "The Lord's Prayer." Her answer was an all-encompassing experience, with no sharp corners, no rough edges. Life flowed. Her words, "The Lord's Prayer" carried him along, and he sensed that life is a stream, the river of God. The rule of life was neither alien nor unknown. It had been given once and for all time in The Lord's Prayer.

*   *   *

THE LORD'S PRAYER

Our Father in heaven,
  hallowed be your Name,

When Jesus spoke these words, he was announcing a whole new approach to the living of human life. He called God, "Abba," father, and so told us that we were not to live at a distance from God but in the most intimate companionship. God was close, approachable, intimate—just as close to us, if we have been lucky, as our own parents.

My own father was the one who gave me life. He was the one in whose image I was made. Our physique and visage, our character and our minds, our use of language and our way of seeing and understanding the world, all made this completely clear to me. Yet this very same father could also be distant, distant at the same moment that I knew his love for me was as demanding as it was gentle. I did not learn this through anything he said, but I sensed he knew exactly what it was like for me to be me. One person in all the world, my father, knew what it was like to be inside my skin. He was my father. I was his son.

Every one of us at some time has a relationship like this. It may be with our mother or father, it may be with a grandparent or a godparent, a first grade teacher, a priest or pastor, but it always exists.

One Christmas my father gave me a teddy bear. Teddy was plump and yellow brown. Each night, we said prayers together, Teddy and Daddy and I. As I grew, one day he said to me, "In the dark and quiet you tell Teddy all your secrets, all those things you never tell anyone else, don't you?"

And I said, "Yes. But how did you know?" All he said was, "I love you."

As intimacy is the mark for our relationship with God, which is grounded in love, so it is the mark of friendship with those persons who have chosen us to love. This is more true in marriage than anywhere else. When the ceremony of marriage is complete, at the very moment when at long last the man and the woman have separated themselves from the families who bore and raised and supported them, and who stand behind and apart from them now, the newly married couple say together the words of The Lord's Prayer. The parents have been put aside. In their place is a new creation, a deeper bond than any we have ever known, and together, they pray for the first time as husband and wife, "Our Father in heaven . . . "

As Kitty marries Levin in Tolstoy's novel, *Anna Karenina,* she thinks about her family and her marriage as an old life ending and a new beginning: "Living the old life, she was horrified at herself, at her utter and unconquerable indifference to her past, to the things, the habits, the people she had loved, who had loved her—to her mother who was grieved by her indifference; to her dear affectionate father, whom she had loved more than anyone else in the world. At one moment she was appalled by this indifference, and at the next she rejoiced at

what had brought it about. She could not think of or
desire anything apart from life with this man; but this
new life was not yet, and she could not picture it, clearly.
There was only anticipation—the dread and joy of the
new and unknown. And now behold, anticipation and
uncertainty, and remorse at repudiating her old
life—were all at an end and the new was beginning."

"He who loves his father or mother more than me
is not worthy of me; . . . and he who does not take his
cross and follow me is not worthy of me." (Mt.10:37-38).
This is one of the most difficult of the sayings of Jesus.
To know the fullness of mature stature in the presence
of God, we must sever the umbilical cord that ties each
of us to our parents. This must happen at the moment
of marriage if it is to succeed, the moment we find
ourselves separate and alone, reaching out and clinging
to the one other human being whom we have chosen
and who has chosen us.

At the beginning of a marriage, there can be a
deep and pervasive sense of loneliness and abandon-
ment. We have left our own families and grafted
ourselves as husband and wife onto the greater family of
God. Yet when we stand alone as a new family, we also
stand together, united by the unseen chain of God's
love, which surrounds and supports us in our inevitable
loneliness. Together and apart, we are God's.

*   *   *

. . . The couple had been married only a month when,
on a clear July morning, she drove her husband to the
pier and he boarded the gray ship to sail away for three
months. They were in a new and strange place, all
alone, their marriage already marked by one death and

now a separation, but on that morning they were brave as he strode from the car and up the gangway with a wave and scarcely a backward glance. To one side stood another couple, an old and weathered Chief Warrant Officer, whose sleeve proclaimed over a quarter century of naval service. The chief held himself erect, but collapsed in his arms, his wife hung limp, her entire body racked with sobs that echoed between the hull of the ship and the wall of the pier. The scene made the newly marrieds very uncomfortable, but it spoke the real truth of a terrible parting. This woman knew the agony of loneliness when the only other person in her life was being taken away for months. The young couple could not cry, for the emotion would have overpowered them. The chief's wife did it for them.

your kingdom come,
your will be done,
    on earth as in heaven.

A marriage is a new creation, part of a new world and a new community, centered in this man and this woman, but belonging to a larger family, the kingdom of God. The marriage becomes an opportunity for the man and the woman to live with one another in God's presence. Through their life together they anticipate the kingdom, as husband and wife bring each other into new being.

*   *   *

. . . Periodically, she would fall in love with him over again, and in cooler phases, knowing it would recur, anticipated it almost as some transcendent ordeal. Living with him, she had come to believe that men and

women are given, seek unawares, the experience they
require for their own particular ignorance, that pain is
not random. She thought often about Michelangelo's
statues that they had seen years ago in Florence in the
first excitement of their love, figures hidden in the block
of stone, uncovered only by the artist's chipping away
the excess, the superficial blur, till smooth and spare, the
true shape is revealed. She and Ivan were hammer and
chisel to each other.

*   *   *

As the marriage begins, everything is expectation.
Nothing yet exists, but everything is in place. These two
people will never be any more married than they are
right now, yet the entire marriage exists only as promise,
a future hope. In the same way every image, every symbol of the New Testament, speaks of a kingdom which
is here in our midst, within each of us, and at the same
time is a promise, a future hope. The full reality of God's
kingdom can never be more fully known than in the
creation of something new and lasting. Marriage is a
partial statement of everything we may know in the
kingdom of God.

Jesus often describes the kingdom of God through
the metaphor of a wedding, particularly the wedding
feast, the gathering about one table of diverse people
who have been brought together for this celebration.
Anyone past the age of twelve remembers such a family
celebration, a time of vivid and lifelong memories. They
are memories of a special time, a time of joy and unity,
when, dressed for celebration, one knew that the excitement, the warmth, the hope, were real.

Yet there was also much uneasiness. Nothing was normal or familiar. Each moment was challenging, unexpected. There was even crisis. "Remember the time when Aunt Margaret was put next to Uncle Henry by mistake! You know what they think of one another? Less than nothing at all, that's what!" And many the time, too many, when the bride's and groom's families never really spoke. They had nothing in common. "Will they ever be able to overcome the barriers? I sure doubt it."

But above all else, the marriage feast is the feast of the Eucharist. It is a time of thanksgiving, the opportunity to be bound together through common memories, common dreams, common vision. Will it ever happen again? Can such a moment as this feast be recaptured in the daily, humdrum life of men and women and their children?

* * *

. . . Time came when the young bride and groom were fully grown. They moved to the house where their children, still in elementary school, would grow up together, but this might never have happened without the intimacy of their meals together. Family meals had been the bond that surrounded and taught this husband and wife as they had grown. The dining room table was the center for all the best learning, both in their childhood and in their life together. At table they met, for better or worse, as husband and wife. Now there were children. Now they were a family.

The woman bought a round blue table for her family to sit at. On the very first night that they sat down together and held hands for grace, she announced that this daily gathering would be known as The Council of the Blue Table. Here the family would gather once a day and share a meal, and here all conversation shared at the blue table would be held in complete confidence. "This family began and continues in Eucharist," she said. "Here we gather in thanksgiving for all we have been given by God to do the daily business that belongs only to this family."

Soon rules were written down by each member of the family, framed, and hung next to the table.

RULES FOR THE BLUE COUNCIL

1. Things said at the table do not go out of the Kitchen.
2. Be honest.
3. No yelling !!
4. <u>EVERYONE</u> shall always be nice and pleasant to Daddy.
5. As long as Daddy behaves himself.
6. Burping and pharting allowed.
7. No swearing.

Give us today our daily bread.

Quite naturally, we assume that this petition for "daily bread" is primarily for the fulfillment of basic physical needs. Nothing else may be achieved in a day or a lifetime unless the need for food and shelter and rest is met. These are minimal needs; without them we can accomplish nothing. Yet this is only the very beginning, because those who lack the most minimal life supports often do so because other supports have been withdrawn. There is, for instance, no family, not a family as most know it. The marriage, troubled as it was, came to an end. Alcohol became first an irritant and then an addiction. Any trace of emotional warmth disappeared for this person, as did any sense of self-worth. Where warmth and a sense of value should have existed, there arose need—need of the most basic and vital kind: the need for food and shelter. Yet the need was far deeper and more pervasive.

*   *   *

. . . Sean was an identical twin, born minutes after his brother, in an Army hospital. His parents' careers in the service brought the family enough financial security to dissolve normal childhood anxieties, but Sean's childhood was fractured, often disrupted, full of dislocations and the frequent change of all that was familiar. "My brother got all the attention. He did nothing wrong, and I did nothing but bad. Mom and dad were at me all the time, 'Do this!' or 'Stop that!' Why, I really can't remember a time when mom hugged me. She just didn't have any time for me."

Posts overseas brought valuable exposure to different cultures, but also removal from the continued, intimate, supportive family love a little boy needed. Tall, blond, winsome and intelligent, Sean suffered from a severe learning disability, undiagnosed by family or teachers. Everything needful was apparently provided, but Sean grew up alone and untouched. By the time he reached twenty-five, he was lost to his family, out on the street, in and out of state institutions, homeless.

*   *   *

In their attempts to breed and raise "the master race" the Nazis created the "perfect" environment to raise Aryan infants, selectively bred. The babies were placed in a sterile and protected place, where highly skilled nurses tended them day and night. One unusual condition prevailed; the new race should not be in any way defiled by human contact of any kind. All the infants' needs were attended without any fondling or cuddling, and all of them died.

This very same deprivation exists in many families and every culture, whenever a child is raised without touch, without embrace, without support. It may well be that every physical need is met, or, on the other hand, the table is bare. The daily bread that this child needs to grow is not bought with money. It comes with touch, and without it, there will be death.

Aside from the daily bread of physical sustenance, there are two other kinds of daily bread, both integral to the fabric of marriage. Each is a bread of warmth, a bread of responsiveness and embrace. Each is a bread to feed the soul with the intimate realization of eternal worth. One is psychic, the other spiritual.

Marriage involves the entire human being. From the new creation comes constant giving and taking, a channel through which strength flows to and from each to the other. It is this which sustains life in its essence, and without it there would cease to be life. It is daily bread—psychic bread. There is one person amongst the many, one person alone, who knows and understands me through and through, and loves me all the same. This knowledge, understanding, and love must be revealed in countless ways, for there are many ways of speaking in marriage.

The Phil Donahue Show, platform for the proclamation of the manners and morals of the United States,
has affirmed that the greatest problem in marriage is
communication. This is as wise as the old saying: "I've
been rich and I've been poor. Rich is better," or as
profound as the finding that most persons prefer the
climate on a Caribbean island to that of Anchorage,
Alaska. Nevertheless it is true. Communication between
two people is a learned skill, an art, which needs constant, daily, hourly practice. It is not an automatic gift
that springs to life once the vows are spoken. Rather the
ability to communicate well emerges through time, expression and response. It is the source of life to those
fortunate to give and receive it, a rich treasure found
only in the kind of friendship afforded by secure
marriage.

*   *   *

. . . It would be impossible to know where to begin to tell
the tale of their friendship and marriage. It stretched
back into time, touching many places and times, countless people. Somehow, they would say, each moment is
continuous with every other, despite variety and distance. Both husband and wife believed it was all bound
together by their constant sense of shared history. This
produced the realization at so many moments, alone
and with others, when he knew precisely what she was
thinking, or she knew, virtually to the word, what he
would say. Then they would laugh at each other and
kiss, or exchange a silent glance across the crowded
room.
    Anger and verbal explosion were well known in
their marriage. These were forms of intimacy, and in-

timacy, once chosen, knows neither boundary nor limit. There was never a moment when husband or wife did not know the power of the love of the other, the love which filled each with the realization that life had a beginning and an end, and right now was marked by the clear reality that each had and held and knew the other through and through. It was to know the meaning of being fed.

*   *   *

There are three forms of daily bread: bread to feed the body, bread to feed the psyche, bread to feed the spirit. Spiritual bread assures and reaffirms our sense of eternal worth. It is the bread of eternal life, which feeds us all. Spiritual bread has a presence all   its own, assuring us again and again of God's love in Christ and our eternal worth. Yet for this bread to fill us, it must be received in a context which allows its meaning to be discovered. For some people, certainly not all, this may happen in childhood through the warmth of parental love. When this love is gone, only one love has the power and presence to carry this message. It is the love of marriage. The experience of married loved enables one to know the power of God's love in the bread of the Eucharist, just as the Eucharist makes it possible to know the complete depth of married love. Both say to us: you are known, and as you are known, you are loved. In our lifetime, there are two who know us through and through. One is God, the other is our spouse.

*   *   *

. . . Most people who knew them certainly would say that they were ordinary people, at best. Background, job, surroundings, accomplishments, even their dreams for the future, were pretty humdrum. But every single morning, day after day, year after year, they awoke in an embrace surrounded by the dark and the quiet. When that happened, whatever the hour, one would say to the other, "I love you." In time, through the fog and sleep of dreams, there would be the reply, "I love you." Sometimes that was all. Sometimes there was conversation, sometimes not. This time of communion set them apart and bound them together.

Through the fabric of this ordinary and very daily life, there was one other time of communion, and it too was repeated very regularly. This was when they knelt together, side by side, at the altar rail, to receive the Body of Christ. That was a very daily bread, ordinary, and it fed them day by day.

Forgive us our sins
  as we forgive those
    who sin against us.
Save us from the time of trial,
  and deliver us from evil.

. . . Once again, it must have been the tenth time this month, she returned home late, more than an hour later than they had agreed on parting that morning. She knew she should be contrite, but she was goddamned if she would apologize. What the hell? Why should he always be so demanding? Who made him a judge over her?

She entered the house as silently as possible, removed her coat, and crept into the living room. The room was dark; there was not a sound anywhere. She shuffled back into the front hall, through the dining room and opened the door to the kitchen. Only the light over the stove was on, and under it she could see the note.

Elizabeth—As far as I am concerned, this is it! We agreed you would return for dinner. I am sick of waiting. John

She ripped up the note, stormed to the liquor cabinet and then to the ice maker and back to make a drink. She swore and almost tore the door off its hinges returning to the living room. She turned on several lights, drew the curtains and sat down next to her drink and the unread part of the newspaper. She sat there for a very long time, getting more and more angry. After all, she earned the larger salary. But all the time he was laying down rules, rules which made no sense. His understanding of what she did and why and who was important in her world was nil. She knew the *really* important people. Maybe life had more to offer than this miserable marriage.

It was midnight and several drinks later when she heard his footstep in the kitchen. She did not move. He walked through the hall and without entering the living room, even he must have known she was there, turned and went upstairs.

She sat alone for another hour before climbing the stairs. He was lying in the bed in the dark, wide awake. Neither said anything for a very long time. Then finally, and with the greatest of difficulty, she said the most difficult words, "I'm sorry." Both burst into tears and clung together. They stayed this way for a long time, unable to speak. When at last they could, they began to talk about time—the time they shared with one another. They talked too about commitment to one another, to his job, to her job, to those parts of their lives separate one from the other. It was a conversation long overdue, a conversation which struck at the core of their marriage, but it never really reached a conclusion, for they were overcome by the sudden freedom to make love, wild—reminiscent of earlier days. Finished and spent, they lay in each others arms, newly sanctified.

"It may sound stupid, Elizabeth, but I just have to tell you how much I love you."

"Me too. Thank you"

*   *   *

The authority which prevails in a marriage is the authority of love. It is an authority unlike any other, because it seeks to understand what it is like to be in the skin of the other person. It is an authority which allows me to value you just as you are, and not for any presumed perfection or ability to conform to my expectations. Forgiveness is the only possible basis for such authority, together with the ability and willingness to let go of pride and self-righteousness and to live with and for one another.

Two people living together in the bond and covenant of marriage will inevitably and regularly hurt one another. The hurt will most often be caused by the simple tendency to assert what I want and who I am at the expense of the other. This is unavoidable and guaranteed. When it happens, we seek to be forgiven, just as we forgive. Otherwise marriage will not survive.

Save us from the time of trial,

Temptation is constant, daily, as is our willingness to succumb to it. Marriage calls us to be open; to be open means to be vulnerable; to be vulnerable is to seek to wound in ways intentional and unintentional, known and unknown, remembered and forgotten, ways as small as being constantly late, as great as having an affair. If by great effort we are able to avoid the temptation to wound, there is always the desire to control our spouse through money or the children or through affection withheld. But when, through the test of time and patience, we should weary of the ability to wound and to control, then we seek to kill one another, for in marriage it can be done with great ease.

*   *   *

. . . So many times, too many, he had watched her watch other men. The other man came in various guises, ages and appeared in the most unexpected places, but his appearance was as regular as the sunrise. He grew to loathe and fear that other man. Loathe him for changing his life, undermining his marriage, fear him for everything which he did not know, did not dare to know and about which he would not even ask. But he allowed it to happen. Never did he interfere or reach out to save her from that other man.

He was too scared. He had watched his mother and father through their mockery of a marriage. It had been little more than a convenience, and he had vowed that this would never happen to him. Now it was happening, unfolding in just the same way, and he was paralyzed. What paralyzed him was fear, fear of who he was.

Even though he was young, he gave serious thought to following in his father's footsteps, who at long last decided to endure his marriage no longer and ended his own life. Planning was careful, covering days and weeks. He weighed options, considered time and place and method, and when the choice was made, he secured the pills from several sources and in large quantity. There would be no mistake, no embarrassing failure.

Before he did it, he had to make a final gesture. It should be more than a gesture, but an act of courage to offer himself fully to face the trial, to meet the evil, face to face. He planned a trip, a time away, just the two of them. Maybe they might be able to meet, to discover one another. They went away; something did begin to happen. There seemed a change; hope kindled. He was more honest, more endearing, more giving than he ever had been. Until he came upon her trying to seduce the strikingly handsome and young headwaiter. Now there was no question. He would do it.

She happened to come across the pills, hidden in his suitcase far at the back of their closet, but refused to believe that she had seen them. In the middle of that very night, he rose, as quietly as possible, swallowed them all, and lay down on the bathroom floor. As he lay there, silent and alone, he knew he didn't want to die. He went to ask his wife for help. As they were rushed to the hospital, their marriage became a possibility for the very first time.

and deliver us from evil.

Evil is not unlike alcoholism. Alcoholism is a disease which tells the alcoholic at every opportunity that he does not have a disease. Human beings refuse to deal

with or understand the presence of evil in their lives
because to do so means to acknowledge human responsibility. Evil results from the human desire to
think of self, to achieve my need to the detriment of
someone else. The more I am unwilling to face the dark
reality, the more it has power over me and the world;
the more I outrageously serve this dark reality, the more
it becomes the single most invidious power in the
world.

So it is that Jesus makes this the final petition in his
prayer. Jesus asks us on a daily basis, whenever we pray,
to be aware that evil exists in the world and to ask God
to deliver us from it. As we ask, and as we mean what
we ask, then, and only then are we empowered to be
delivered from the evil which lurks always, like a wild
beast, within our own breasts and outside our own
doors. It is good gone awry, assertiveness turned against
self and the other. It may become rampant, infectious,
feeding and growing on itself, a cancer, a disease, within
us and all around us.

At the end of Edmund Fuller's novel, *The Corridor*,
a story of the redemptive power of marriage, the husband and wife have gone to the midnight Eucharist, the
first Mass of Christmas. Lying in bed afterwards in the
early hours of Christmas morning, the husband reflects:

"As he lay beside her in the calm darkness he pondered
the enigma of being in love—the faith and commitment
provable only in a continuum of time and act. It took
much time and many acts, long past the flush of romantic attraction, to learn to love someone for *being*, not
for the ebb and flow of services and amenities. In the
love for being were absorbed and assimilated all the

clashes, frictions, sins, irritants and cross purposes of any long association and any growing family. . .

"I know nothing of marriage in the abstract, he reflected. I know only one marriage and its intense reality. The passing shames, the lacerations that had marked the trail of this marriage were not obliterated. They were deposits in his mind. They prevented him from falling prey to the illusion that the problems of marriage were over, as if their new lease on life were somehow in the New Jerusalem and not in the hard terrain outside the eastern gates of the Garden.

"There would be pain and laceration again, in one form or another, and they would do well if they did not crack with it. He did not know what the problems would be, but he felt he knew in what directions the solutions would lie. He knew nothing of the answers that were inadmissable, of the alleys that were blind. He thought, with gently sardonic remembrance of a simpler romanticism. We are not the ideal married couple. We are—God help us—man and woman."

*   *   *

. . . If ever there were times—and there were, frequently—when nothing seemed to make sense, no sense at all, there was always one thing which held it all together. That was their marriage.

Long ago it had become evident that this did not mean that everything was perfect. Far from it. In fact that was just the point. They both knew there would continue to be terror and loneliness and brokenness and pain. It would exist all around them, and they would create their own share merely by living with and for one another. That was to be expected. It was an integral part, sometimes it seemed to be the integral part, even the only part, of human life. This was not a surprise. Yet when the night was darkest, and there was no hope, no hope at all, then light broke through. Lost and lonely as they were or had become and would always be, they reached across the dark and found one another.

*   *   *

Years ago Arthur Miller sat down to write the story of his own marriages. The two which had broken and died, forever, and the third which lives and breathes in and through its brokenness. And there, as he concluded his own story, Miller said of marriage:

"To know, and even happily, that we meet unblessed; not in some garden of wax fruit and painted trees, that lie of Eden, but after, after the Fall, after many, many deaths . . . "

So few of us ever realize it, even those who know better. We forget that life is not perfection and was never intended to be. And so Miller reminds us that marriage is an opportunity, the adventure of two ordinary persons. It is an opportunity to celebrate that ordinariness and in finding and meeting it to transform everything we know, everything we care about, and everything we ever experience into something more. It is the something more hinted at in the design in the tapestry. It is the something more proclaimed by Jesus in the words of the prayer he taught us to pray. It is the something more which we do not merely glimpse, but grasp in the arms of one another in the dark of the night when we know with a lasting certainty that if nothing else matters, one thing does. It is what we have and hold and love and cherish right now, together.

For the kingdom, the power,
  and the glory are yours,
    now and for ever. Amen

THEIR COMMON LIFE

THE PRAYERS

The business for which everyone has gathered, the marriage, is nearly concluded. Relief. People begin to stir, look around. Some cease to listen, if indeed they ever did, while the newly married couple realize they have nothing to do but listen. The prayers of the marriage unfold and offer a chance for them to reflect, look ahead, to form a picture of their common life.

These prayers describe the context of marriage—grace. Grace is not a familar concept. The American Way is marked by go-go-go, get-get-get, climb-climb-climb. Our lives are symbolized by elevators or escalators. The games we play are "leap-frog" and "who did you know" or "guess who I saw on the way to the..." Marriage we are told, on the other hand, depends on

Eternal God, creator and preserver of all life, author of salvation, and giver of all grace: Look with favor upon the world you have made, and for which your Son gave his life, and especially upon this man and this woman whom you make one flesh in Holy Matrimony. Amen.

At the heart of marriage is grace.

Grace is serendipitous, grace is unexpected, grace is unearned, a gift offered without reason but never without need. Grace is that moment between two persons which heals and binds in the twinkling of an eye, real and memorable, but never lasting. Grace comes and grace goes; without grace life would not be possible.

Marriage is built upon grace; marriage depends upon grace. It is not a contract that depends upon the exchange of goods and services, based upon what each does to and for the other. Marriage is a condition of being, not doing. Marriage is based on who we are one with another. Marriage lives and grows with grace, and without grace marriage dies.

Grace within marriage is more available than in any other relationship. Grace is present when we say "I love you" for no reason beyond the welling up of pure emotion, when she comes home early just so they can have an extra hour together, or he tells her that the work in his briefcase is not as important as the long conversation at the kitchen table. Grace feeds itself. One moment occasions and then strengthens another. Grace is the force which knits human beings together in a web more powerful than intellect and more lasting than knowledge. Grace is the glue of marriage, the stuff from which marriage is created, the single power of new life and constant growth.

*   *   *

. . . The sun was shining, but for him it was a dark, grim day. Nothing was worthwhile, he thought, everything was begun, continued and concluded only by the most significant and unpleasant effort.

Somehow all that changed the moment his friend, Ned, stopped by. There seemed to be no reason for his presence, yet he remained. Conversation strayed from Ned's casual inquiry about the book he misplaced right here last week, to a lengthy description of the essay he had just completed, to concern for a mutual friend. Somehow, through this conversation about things which each of them took seriously, ran a common thread—their daily work was necessary and important.

The visit ended as suddenly as it had begun. When it was over, he realized that in that twinkling of an eye everything had changed, it was all worthwhile. He left his office, whistling, on the way to the meeting he had dreaded.

Returning home for supper, when he kissed his wife hello, she asked with no special emphasis, "Oh, did Ned find you in your office this afternoon? He happened to walk by as I was working outside, and I asked if he had a moment to stop by and see you. I said you needed cheering up."

Give them wisdom and devotion in the ordering of their common life, that each may be to the other a strength in need, a counselor in perplexity, a comfort in sorrow, and a companion in joy. Amen.

"Give them wisdom and devotion in the ordering of their common life," may easily be translated to the less poetic but accurate statement: "May they be friends." The prayer then goes on to state quite specifically that husband and wife be very close and special friends, bound together one to another in need, perplexity, sorrow and joy.

The fact is often overlooked that those who are married one to another are first, last, and always best friends. There is no other person in the world with whom each would rather be. In the strict economy of time, more must be invested in and with the other than with any other single human being. Friendship is built upon and grows with the investment of time. "Quality" time does not make up for the constant and increasing quantity of time spent together. Then and only then will each be to the other "a strength in need, a counselor in perplexity, a comfort in sorrow, and a companion in joy."

The professional counselor is sought out and paid by the hour not so much for advice, as we like to think, but for concern. The counselor is the paid lover of society, and some are paid more than others, yet the concern and affirmation sought through professional counsel are more readily, easily and ably available in marriage. What each of us needs is not a paid lover, but the lover who is our spouse. It is in marriage that we may find strength, counsel, comfort and companionship. This is our common life.

Grant that their wills may be so knit together in your will, and their spirits in your Spirit, that they may grow in love and peace with you and one another all the days of their life. Amen.

. . . The marriage had grown richer through thirty years, as had their investment of shared history, common memories, endless days and hours. More and more it was natural for each to think one's own thoughts after the other. Once the topic of conversation had been introduced, even before any word was uttered, either might begin, knowing with some precision what the other was thinking. Questions would be answered before being asked, only summoned to consciousness. It didn't matter where they were—riding in the car, sitting at table, preparing for bed or making plans for the weekend, there was a level of communication which supported and enveloped them.

This communion was a form of prayer. Sometimes it was wordless, often it took the form of casual conversation, and at other times it was heated argument. Sometimes they would say the Lord's Prayer together, sometimes it was a few words before a meal. Prayer resulted from their closeness, but prayer also created it.

*   *   *

The word of salvation and the act of redemption will not find each of us from some far distant and unknown source. It will meet us in the midst of the marriage.

*   *   *

. . . The Sunday had been a normal one, if indeed any day had been normal in the past month. They had been living in the midst of a great tension, the tension of loss and silence. The tension came from the pretense that nothing had changed. Only everything had changed. Surrounded by the emptiness, they tried to understand why they had uprooted themselves, left the only home they knew to move to a strange city. Not even the children were with them. She had not found a job. They felt as if they were living through and beyond their own death.

It was exactly five o'clock in the afternoon when he finally mentioned that he did not feel quite himself. As he walked from the kitchen to the bedroom to lie down, she heard him say, "I don't feel too peppy." It seemed as if he had a chill, for he shook all over, hyperventilated several times. She covered him with the quilt. They were not looking at each other, but he could sense her anxiety and helplessness. Here they were, alone, in a new place, a new world, the future uncertain, everything unknown.   What if he really were sick? Where was help?

She made him put on a sweater and held him for an hour. Neither slept. Nothing changed.   But at six he made himself rise from the bed. He had no strength and did not speak but walked from room to room, and she followed. Suddenly, for no particular reason she embraced him and he her.   And then he started to cry, deep wracking sobs, uncontrollable. "You have held it all in for far too long. Let it out. Let it out."

His wild sobbing stopped, as suddenly as it had begun. He went to sit on the living room couch. Then lay down.   Why it happened, even what had happened, was not important, only that she joined him, hugged him, and then the sobs began again. She understood.

Once she had made a pot of coffee and brought it in, they sat and talked on the couch for two hours. His crying was over. Now they sorted it out.   The symptoms had been released. Resolution had come, occasioned by her touch, her voice, her love, which healed him.

Give them grace, when they hurt each other, to recognize and acknowledge their fault, and to seek each other's forgiveness and yours. Amen.

"Be angry but do not sin; do not let the sun go down on your wrath" (Eph. 4:26).   We tend to remember the second half of this quotation but forget the first, "Be angry but do not sin."   It speaks of a constant reality in marriage, for there is no such thing as friendship, no such thing as love, no such thing as marriage without anger.   A thin line separates love from anger, but the opposite of love is not anger, but indifference. Anger is strong and fierce and burns bright with heat and passion. So too does love, and they are often closely intertwined.

"Be angry but do not sin." Anger is one thing, sin quite another. The use of the word here is neither mysterious nor unusual. Be angry, but do not nurse the anger, do not sulk, do not use the anger to draw the world into yourself. Do not be angry always and only to gain the advantage, to prevail, to win the argument.

*   *   *

. . . The middle child always sat to his left at the family table. Mealtime in their family was meant to be the occasion for frank and honest talk. Sometimes emotions ran high. One evening, as had been known to happen in the past, conflict emerged between father and child. She was eleven, strong-willed, outspoken, verbal, intelligent; most of all she was explosive. On this occasion, as she burst into tears, however, she sat still, and said to her father with great strength of purpose: "I've figured you out. You make a point, get angry and raise your voice. Then I cry, get up, run to my room and slam the door, and you win. This time it's going to be different. I'm staying right here until I win."
      She did.

Give them grace, when they hurt each other, to recognize and acknowledge their fault, and to seek each other's forgiveness and yours. Amen.

Anger is important and even necessary, but it is a means of honest expression, not a weapon. If it becomes a weapon, then it will turn back upon the one who uses it and destroy unless love intervenes. This prayer states that each will hurt the other; this is expected. But when this happens, the hope is that God's grace may allow each to recognize and acknowledge fault and seek forgiveness. Live through it, and then leave it.

When there is no marriage, then there is no anger, there is no fighting, there is no disagreement. Life is flat, uneventful, unpunctuated by change, upheaval, alteration of mood and response. Marriage that is living and breathing and full of the real stuff of life knows every change of mood. Even when those moods are unpleasant and unwelcome, the only thing more unwelcome is their total absence.

Little children, who grow up surrounded by the warmth of a strong marriage, often express fear and disapproval when parents fight. " Stop that. You keep fighting, and you'll get a divorce!" They have heard from children who live with nothing but continual parental conflict that fighting results in divorce. Sometimes it does. The complete absence of anger, however, will more often cause marital distance never to be overcome. Anger is an integral part of love.

It is too often stated by married couples who reach an amicable divorce agreement that they can not recall the last time they had a fight. The distance which grows up between them, a distance created by a total lack of feeling, amazes them.

*   *   *

. . . This fight, like all the others, had been about something small and stupid. They each knew what it was, all right, and it seemed terribly important at the time. What was really important was what each had invested of self into such a small, insignificant thing: the choice of toilet paper.

It had all escalated rapidly and soon the history and value of his and her family, and background, even their parents' professions were at stake. Not long after that, it seemed that even their marriage itself was at stake. Still no one backed down. Each continued to push for advantage.

Exhaustion at long last brought the battle to an end. Silence followed, deathly silence, silence which was meant to kill, and it did.

The days flowed on as if all were normal. He found it possible to maintain himself by his common routine, until finally everything fell apart for him. Late one night in their bed surrounded by the dark, he lost all perspective. Spatial relationships were gone. Nothing made sense. Over and over again, for no reason, he cried out, "I am weak and little and lonely and lost. I am weak and little and lonely and lost." Nothing made sense or mattered or had value, nothing. It was as if he were psychotic. He was totally aware of who he was and what he was saying and why. It was all crazy, but there was nothing he could, or wanted to do, to change any of it.

The sensation was what he imagined it might feel like to fall through space. It was dark, and he was floating, downward. Down, down, down. The dark became darker still. Powerlessness overcame him. And then she caught him.

For no reason, no reason at all, good or bad, she reached out through the dark and touched him, softly, gently, and said, "I'm sorry. It was all so stupid. You know how much I love you." He did not think he could speak, but somehow he heard himself say the same, "I'm sorry. It was all so stupid. You know how much I love you."

What happened next is not easily described. Anger and loss and total desperation had seemed final, but that finality had been faced. Now it was overcome. N o warning, none at all, controlled by passion, fused as one, their world became a kaleidoscope, and formed in brilliant colors all they knew. The act of love was more passionate than either could remember.

Make their life together a sign of Christ's love to this sinful and broken world, that unity may overcome estrangement, forgiveness heal guilt, and joy conquer despair. Amen.

This prayer harkens back to the words of The Exhortation, asking that this marriage may be the very embodiment of the Church, the sign of Christ's love. Here on earth, God's work surely is our own. The person of Jesus is God in human flesh; those who are baptized into Christ's name are the embodiment of Jesus' presence in this world. Marriage in the name of Christ is the expression of Christ's love to a sinful and broken world.

Christ came to this world because it is sinful and broken. Our own desire to center everything around the self separates us from one another and from God and even from our own essential identity. We are not who we want to be, or even who we might be.

In a broken world one union carries more hope and promise than any other, the union of man and woman in marriage. Here potential becomes reality. Here separation can be overcome, forgiveness brings healing and new life, replacing guilt and shame. Here there is joy, because the life of two people, together, has hope and a future.

*   *   *

. . . It was never an ideal marriage, if there is such a
thing. They met at a house party while she was still in
college, and he was in graduate school. The courtship
was passionate, wild. In three months they were married
and off to the first job. She worked in the city and
became pregnant too soon—too soon that is, to allow the
marriage to grow. The first child was followed, again too
soon, by a second, and then a move and than a promotion and then a new and unfriendly city. He worked
hard, too hard, was too seldom at home, but after all,
one did not get ahead by being a good husband.

The third child did not survive birth, and the
mother almost died. She was still recovering when the
father went off to bury the small white casket, accom-
panied only by his parents. Soon there was yet another
upheaval, another move to a new place, brought about
by promotion and new opportunity. The ladder was
moving rapidly, upward, and he was going with it. The
American Dream.

Some of the dream was a nightmare. Death of
parents, serious illness, two affairs, his and hers, never
enough money, the constant demands of job and career.
The children grew up as strangers to one another and
their parents, seldom home, never time for conversation or for one another. Then came the father's
mid-life crisis, which threatened to carry everything
away, as if the marriage and family had never been. If
this is a horror story, what else is new? For this is a
parable of many a marriage in our time.

Yet there was one difference. Magic solutions were
neither sought nor provided. Through it all, each spouse
held on to the other. It worked. There was nothing

unusual. These were ordinary people, but people who never gave up on one another nor on their marriage. They were married, very. The world *is* broken, but unity does overcome estrangement, and forgiveness does heal guilt, and joy does conquer despair. Why? The answer is simple. Marriage is based on a vow, and in the midst of that vow is Christ.

Bestow on them, if it is your will, the gift and heritage of children, and the grace to bring them up to know you, to love you, and to serve you. Amen.

Children do not make a marriage, in fact they may pose the most serious threat a marriage faces, but should there be children in the marriage, then they are implicitly present from the moment of the vows and this prayer asks God's blessing for them.

The prayer is optional, but those who omit it live to regret the choice. They avoid the clear reality that the decision of whether or not to have children is an essential part of marriage. No healthy marriage rests solely upon the children, and if it does it is in trouble, but children, present or absent, are part of the fabric of marriage. Children are the shared creation of the marriage, the living embodiment of two individual identities which have become one flesh.

Children are a gift and a heritage; we bequeath them to the future when everything else has disappeared. Ironically, the two most important opportunities allowed to human beings—marriage and parenthood—are undertaken with little or no preparation, and this is a a reality which each one of us must confront. When Paul Tsongas, then the able and popular junior Senator from Massachusetts, decided to retire from public office and devote the majority of his life to wife and children, he was reminded of the wise words of an old friend: "No one ever said on his death bed, 'I wish I'd spent more time at my business.'" Yet again and again, with depressing regularity, both men and women place their chief emphasis on vocation, both in preparation and pursuit. This pursuit too often robs children. One hour devoted to one child will be remembered years later, while the one hour spent at work last Thursday afternoon—no matter how worthy—will be completely forgotten next week. The opportunity to devote time to one's own children has been abandoned, either by necessity or choice, to thrust oneself into the workplace and to say to oneself, too late, "I wish I'd spent more time with my children."

*   *   *

The eldest child of the family recalled one of her earliest memories.

"My father was a minister, and I remember standing behind him braiding the fringe on his stole, watching as he shook people's hands after church, ducking behind him as they reached to pinch my cheek or pat my head, all the while feeling proud and secure in knowing my father was somehow important and good.

"That was Washington in the early 1960's. My mother volunteered in the D.C. ghettos and would later start a Headstart in our small New Hampshire town. I remember my father went to hear Martin Luther King, Jr. deliver his 'I Have a Dream' speech. I remember going to J.F.K.'s graveside the day he was buried. As I looked down at the burning flame over the grave from my father's shoulders, I didn't understand, but I knew something was wrong.

"Later we moved to a school community, where my father was the school minister. It was a time of turmoil, the late Sixties. My parents led peace marches through the town and later to Washington. I remember a student staggering through our house on an LSD trip looking for my mother to help him . . . the minister from Biafra crying in the living room . . . visiting my mother when she worked with mentally handicapped children.

"From an early age my parents talked to us about the importance of service, helping others, making a difference. From my childhood perspective I could see the difference they made in the lives of others—the students who would always write, come back and visit, the many close friends and colleagues, the enthusiastic responses to my father's sermons.

Mine was a very warm and nurturing childhood. My parents were very sensitive to our needs and concerns. There was an emphasis placed on the importance of family, trust, and honest and open communication. As I entered adolescence, I began to realize that this warmth and caring I had experienced was more unique than ordinary. The more I came to this realization, the more I sought to share what I had known with others."

Give them such fulfillment of their mutual affection that they may reach out in love and concern for others. Amen.

This prayer is skillful and accurate. It assumes that married persons will be such a source of mutual affection, one for the other, that there will be an outpouring of love and concern to all those who move in the orbit of their love. More than all else, marriage becomes the possibility for Christ to be present in this center of strength, which will grow to be an expression of love to

the world. Love begets love. The loving response not
only turns away wrath, but is the occasion for greater
love. Marriage is the expression of love which wel-
comes and embraces, accepts and approves. The power of
this affection reaches out to embrace, to console and to
heal.

*   *   *

. . . It was a moment that both of them would always
remember. They were staying as guests in a strange city
with a couple whom they had never met. They had
come for a job interview, which made each moment
even more nerve-wracking, since everyone involved
was looking over everyone else.

The house was formal, Victorian; it put them on
their guard. Breakfast would be served at eight, they
were told. Knowing the anxiety that morning would
bring, their night was far from restful; they stayed awake
for most of it, whispering between twin beds. Finally
dawn came, and they rose, dressed and, feeling haggard,
came downstairs. The four sat together around the table,
and, without warning, their host made an unexpected
request. Reaching out to clasp hands around the table,
he began the words of the Lord's Prayer, followed by a
blessing, asking for God's presence throughout the
coming day. From this moment the atmosphere
changed. The guests felt at home and at one with the
people whose hands they had held.

Conversation warmed and relaxed as they asked and
were told how the host and hostess met, courted, and
moved, as a newly married couple, to this great and new
and strange city. It was she who spoke. He smiled
quietly, as if agreeing.

"We both came to this city from other places. We knew no one here. But when we married and moved, we promised one another that our love would make it possible to work together to make our life together matter, matter for good, matter for other people, matter for those things which are important to us: church, family, education, justice. That choice has been behind everything I have tried to do for the schools of this county, the establishment of educational television, our work for racial justice, my husband's role in the one man-one vote decision, our commitment to our church —all these have been ways we have experienced Christ's love in the marriage we have been given."

Something happened right then, all at once, which brought the strangers into the circle of love and commitment which lived in that house.

Grant that all married persons who have witnessed these vows may find their lives strengthened and their loyalties confirmed. Amen.

Everyone present at the wedding needs to be reminded that such vows, once undertaken, must be constantly renewed. The endurance of every marriage depends upon the constant reinforcement of the power and purpose of the marriage vows. The strengthening and affirmation of marriage must also be sought and welcomed continually from every kind of outside source.

*   *   *

. . . We arrived early for the wedding and sat nestled next to a large pillar in the center of the church. A young woman, wearing a dress made from bed ticking, was already seated behind us; she was reading from the Book of Common Prayer. As the church filled, rapidly and noisily, she was joined, first by one old friend and then a second.   Their reunion was loud. Conversation, impossible not to overhear, told us that they had been at school with the maid of honor, who was the sister of the bride.

The procession began, and, as we awaited the entrance of the bride, the last of the four friends arrived. Flashy, very short black hair, dressed in very chic white, she said to her friends: "Marriage.. . . . marriage! Stan and I think about it all the time, but right now, where would we find the time? Stan and I each spend twenty-four hours a day, I mean, literally, six days a week, taping our music. It is so exhausting, but so worthwhile. God, is it worthwhile. There just is no time for anything else. But we have it so good. *Nothing* could be better!"

The non-stop conversation which continued right through the ceremony made it clear that all three had indeed come to witness this wedding, but each had little interest in marriage—neither this one nor her own. It was also clear that each had come planning to spend this time together examining, evaluating, and confirming the vows and loyalties upon which they had based their lives.   When all the tapes had been finished, the modeling career ended, and the bank job lost through merger, then what would happen?

*   *   *

Too often the guests at a wedding stand like sticks, transfixed, gazing into space, waiting for the reception and the champagne. But the real business is here and now, and not merely for the woman and the man,

standing together up front.   It is for you and me, who
stand here, together, after five or ten or fifteen or fifty
years. These words, this emphasis, this place and God's
presence is also for us, our vows, our lives, our loyalty
— one to another. Those forces which weaken this fabric
are many and powerful and frequent. This is a moment
to allow us to grow together once again.

*   *   *

. . . At no time was this clearer to them than the
afternoon they stood together, holding tight to each
other, as their daughter was married. This was   a
memory of a lifetime, and it was very right. How much
they prayed for the two who stood before them, prayed
that this couple, now being married   might know the
depth and breadth of love which they had known.

But they prayed too for something else, something
each knew without asking or telling the other. They
prayed for a new beginning, a new level of intimacy in
their knowing of one another. They prayed that their
marriage would continue to become deeper and
stronger. Even as they prayed, they knew it would be.

*Grant that the bonds of our common humanity, by
which all your children are united to one another, and
the living to the dead, may be so transformed by your
grace, that your will may be done on earth as it is in
heaven; where, O Father, with your Son and the Holy
Spirit, you live and reign in perfect unity, now and for
ever.   Amen.*

At this point in the prayers a memory is invoked of
the most ancient moment of the Eucharist, the Sanctus.
At that instant, we are bound to all persons throughout

all of time and space. It is not a common experience, mystical, a time when we realize that we are not alone, but united to the others, who stand in this room, and also to all people, the living and the dead. In such a moment the presence and power of all the saints, all those persons who have died in God's love, are brought together in one, and we know that we are one with them.

If God can bring to pass the most impossible thing we can imagine, which is the blending of two strong, intractable, selfish individuals into one flesh, then can not this same God forge the bonds of our common humanity? The cloud of witnesses which surround the newly married couple are not merely those who stand here together, proclaiming and praying their strong support, but those who have gone before and gather with us here and now at this altar.

*   *   *

. . . The groom, his father, who would be best man, and the priest stood together in the sacristy awaiting the opening chords of Purcell's Trumpet Voluntary, which would signal the wedding procession and the moment to move toward the chancel steps. There was no chit chat, but a good deal of serious prayer. Suddenly, the groom broke the silence with "Damn!" as he snapped his fingers. "We should have a chair out there for grandmother right next to where we'll stand. I mean, I know it will be empty, Amah's dead, but I want to be reminded that she's right here with us."

More silence. Then his father and the priest said, almost in unison. "Amah will be there, Bill. She wouldn't be anywhere else."

THE THINGS WHICH REMAIN

THE BLESSING OF THE MARRIAGE

At this moment husband and wife kneel to receive the blessing. The first of the two blessings summarizes Christian marriage and claims that the Christian faith pervades all of life. Verging often on the poetic, evoking the mythical, calling forth abundant images from our rich past, it ties together the strands of history, common and personal, which bring us now to this moment: the very beginning of the marriage of this man and this woman in the name of Christ.

Most gracious God, we give you thanks for your tender love in sending Jesus Christ to come among us, to be born of a human mother, and to make the way of the cross to be a way of life.

Marriage is one image of the way of the cross. Both are rooted in passion, passion which is life-giving. This is passion which knows that suffering is unavoidable. This is passion which is prepared to undergo anything on behalf of the beloved, for it knows that then and only then will transformation and new life occur.

The cross stands at the center of the Christian faith just as love stands at the center of human life. Both require the giving up of self. In the cross lies the essence of what responds to our deepest fears and anxieties. Here is the key to mystery, the very definition of what it means to live. The cross proclaims that there is no meaning to human life unless it is lived with and for and through others. The cross proclaims that try as we may, as much as we pray, there is no escape from the shared pain of marriage, pain which opens the way to new and deeper fellowship. The cross proclaims that the mark of life is passion. The way of the cross is the daily, the ordinary. This reality has been made clear again and again as we have passed through this liturgy, and now, at the very end, it is restated.

*   *   *

. . . The day began in the dark. Just a few days ago, there had been such hope and promise. That had all ended, without warning, when the cruel, unwarranted, and unannounced blow struck. Nothing could be done. Neither could help the other. The business they ran together, their livelihood, even their house—all lost. Every cent they had was tied up in the business the husband and wife had started from scratch. It was a catastrophe. Nothing mattered, everything was gone.

Then, as so often in the past, for each of them there was the other. Not that the other could ever fix it or make it all right, but at least the other was there when everything else was lost. Because the other was there, and for no other reason, things began to knit together. It was an opportunity for him to offer himself to her, for her to pour out whatever she had to give, even to give it up, if he needed it more. Even that day contained the seeds of new life, which provided new perspective, new hope.

*By the power of your Holy Spirit, pour out the
abundance of your blessing upon this man and this
woman. Defend them from every enemy. Lead them
into all peace. Let their love for each other be a seal
upon their hearts, a mantle upon their shoulders, and a
crown upon their foreheads.*

Bless them in their work and in their companionship;

Before two people are married, each has twenty-
four hours in the day. Together, but still unmarried,
they have forty-eight. After they are married, however,
there are twenty-four hours in their married day, which
belong to both of them together. Those hours represent
their married time, their vocational time, their leisure
time. This is the time they share, and time is a crucial
symbol and commodity, even more so than money,
carefully defined and limited, not to be either wasted or
committed without both of them knowing it.

Married couples who rarely see each other tend to
say, "We have little time together, but the time we
spend is 'quality' time." They may say the same thing
about their children. There is no such thing as "quality
time." All time is of even quality, by definition, and if
we invest more in some hours than in others, then we
rob ourselves and our marriage. The basic unit is time,
and for one to know another and to continue to live and
grow and to know more of the other, there must be time
invested.

in their sleeping and in their waking;

One of the greatest gifts of marriage is the
opportunity daily, nightly, to sleep with one another.
The use of the euphemism "to sleep together" to mean

sexual intercourse is a misuse of language. Sexual intercourse is only one deeply important and exciting result
of sleeping together, even though that proximity, relaxation, privacy and nakedness over and over does lead to
great intimacy and more sexual expression. But there is
more to sleeping together than that.

Sleeping together is the opportunity to communicate throughout the night in every way, even beyond
and beneath the verbal. Wife and husband are bound
together as no two persons can be under any other
imaginable conditions. So sleep provides the occasion
for intimate, disconnected talk in the half state of sleep
or when fully awake in the midst of the night, which
otherwise would just never occur. Marriage comes to
fruition in sleep, the time that precedes and prepares for
the day that will separate and the evening that will
bring them together.

When we calculate the productive hours of the
week, we always omit the hours of sleep. Not so for
those who are married. Long alert conversation may
take place under the cover of total darkness between
three and four o'clock. Words often erupt from one
dreaming and sleeping partner to the other; inter-
connection and interdependence are known at the
deepest level.

*   *   *

. . . Again we sat up late at night in bed, whispering in
the dark, hypnagogic murmurs on the fine line of
consciousness; we felt born from the same soil, our cells
interchangeable. . . Even to say "I love you" was a
semantic error, too great a separation.

in their joys and in their sorrows; in their life and in their death.

The pattern of joy and sorrow has intervened at more than one place throughout the marriage liturgy. While death has been mentioned more than once, until now it has not appeared side by side with life. Marriage is undertaken, and God's blessing implored, "in their life and in their death."

There is little question what is meant by "life" in marriage; virtually every word and nuance and thought of this liturgy apply to abundant life. Yet now we are told that the state of marriage exists also at our death. Inevitably the final moments, the parting of one living member from the other, are summoned to mind. One flesh is to be rended asunder, and even in that rending, the two persons are one in the marriage created by God. At the moment of final parting they will be married, as they have always been, yet what will happen after that?

*   *   *

. . . Only after it was clear that his death would occur within the year did we come to know one another well. We spent countless, important hours together as he struggled to forestall his inevitable death and stay alive, and during all those days we both searched for words to say to each other and to God. Mostly, we laughed. When we were not laughing, we talked about our marriages.

It was not fair that he died; it never is. All who knew him miss him still. Every time I saw her, after he was gone, she still wore the ring, the sign of their vow. Until one day it was gone, and I wanted to ask why, why had she removed it, only I knew. She would have told

me that there are no marriages in heaven, and he was in
heaven, where one day they would again meet.

I am thinking this morning of the beauty of the earth
as you and I both loved it, wondering
how my vision is still half yours—the broken surf
of morning over landforms; slant light; rolling thunder
at the end of our summer picnics; the high dancing
flight of sandhill cranes, their cry that echoed
like water rippling over smooth stones, over the far
        expanse of
bright air. Within and all around us time flowed,
making, unmaking mountains: the crystal essence
still glitters in the sand grains of dry rivers.
Nothing seems lost—light's changes, windswept silence,
the arid land reflecting the shape of water.
I gather pebbles feeling your quiet presence
companion me still in all we loved together.

*Finally, in your mercy, bring them to that table where
your saints feast for ever in your heavenly home;
through Jesus Christ our Lord, who with you and the
Holy Spirit lives and reigns, one God, for ever and ever.*

Marriage takes place in the context of the Eucharist.
It binds together everyone present in one body, and
offers a promise now of what awaits in eternity. So this
marriage, a special vehicle of God's grace, looks forward
to the heavenly banquet in which we shall all be one
flesh. For while there may be no marriages in heaven,
what awaits us at that table is a love which binds us all
in ways we have never known or imagined. All we can
say is that the closest taste of that heavenly banquet we
may know this side of eternity is in marriage. As we
undertake that marriage, we do so surrounded by the

symbols, the foretaste, and the reality of that table where the saints feast forever. Husband and wife are bound in vow and in the promise of bread and wine, the body and blood of him who died so that we might find new life in and with and for one another.

O God, you have so consecrated the covenant of marriage that in it is represented the spiritual unity between Christ and his Church: Send therefore your blessing upon these your servants, that they may so love, honor and cherish each other in faithfulness and patience,

What is the most essential quality of marriage? There are many—most—who say, "communication." It is just that appeal - someone who "really" understands me—that leads many to search out the "other" man or woman. The appeal is real, it is exciting, it is tempting. Why just the other day, or was it last year or will it be next week, an old friend telephoned (he really did and will again) and told me he was leaving his wife for another woman, for that particular other woman was the person who really understood him as his wife never had. They had not been able to talk, he and his wife, really talk, for years, if ever. Sure, everyone knows why communication is so important in marriage.   No question.

But the essential quality of marriage is faithfulness. Communication in every kind of setting ebbs and flows, comes and goes, although it tends to improve if one is faithful. Finally, only one thing makes marriage possible—fidelity. Fidelity is the expression of what the biblical writer meant when he wrote of the man and the woman becoming "one flesh."

Fidelity is rooted in intercourse—not merely in sexual intercourse, but in the intimate relationship of two quite different, even opposite, human beings. Intercourse could not take place without difference, but this difference is enveloped by deep and abiding friendship, expressed in responsiveness, one to the other. Each person sparks the other, calls into being from the other what otherwise would not be. Fidelity is the conviction of the centrality of marriage.

Years ago, a well-known freelance journalist endured and survived a divorce. In her new and single state she decided to combine profession with experience and write a book that analyzed and detailed marriages that worked, marriages that survived, all kinds of marriages. She interviewed countless numbers of couples of all varieties and backgrounds and chose six, all decidedly different, as representative. She told the story of their lives together in a narrative which combined their answers to her series of questions, but always concluded with the same final, the ultimate, question: why? Why did your marriage work? Always the same answer from each and every couple: because we were faithful to one another.

If faithfulness makes marriage possible, then what makes faithfulness possible? Patience. The pairing of these two qualities is as fascinating as it is insightful. Patience involves time, the ability to wait, the knowing that nothing happens without this element of waiting. It understands that life, has a dimension beyond the particular instant. Nothing worthwhile is created in a moment. Creation takes time. Marriage is a creation that depends on patience, and patience makes faithfulness possible. Unless there is faithfulness and patience, then there will be no marriage at all.

* * *

. . . She often thought about time. Everyone did. The bumper stickers: "TGIF" or "One bad day fishing is better than the best day working." Too many conversations mention "killing time"—what a terrible thought—or "whiling away an hour or two," the generally indifferent stance towards time as if it were nothing, except by those who claim that "time is money."

Time is the most complex idea with which we have to deal every day of our lives, willy-nilly. The dimensions, the meaning, the understanding of time can never be fully defined, but time remains.

Old pundits say: "Show me check book stubs, and I'll show you what really matters." She knew better. Show me a calendar, how a person spends every hour of each day, and I'll tell you what really matters most, even more than money. Time is the test. The test of marriage is time.

in wisdom and true godliness, . . .

Wisdom is the ability to ask the difficult question and to realize that it might not have an answer, that it might never have an answer. Wisdom is about as far as we can go. The symbol of wisdom in more than one culture is the owl. That same owl is also the symbol of death. "You know too much for your own good." Wisdom must be tempered. "Be wise as serpents, but innocent as doves." Wisdom is tempered by godliness. "You, therefore, must be perfect, as your heavenly Father is perfect." Godliness is being perfect; it is a dimension of wisdom. It all ties together. Life is a whole. Marriage is at the very center.

*   *   *

. . . Her husband was helpless without her. He may have
been a famous scholar, eloquent, a much-published
author, but it was she who made the marriage work, a
marriage that had never been easy. Crippled in both legs
and unable to move without help, she made everything
flow around her with grace wherever she was, for she
was one of those people who could bring others out of
themselves, enabling them to meet each other. Her
remarks and insight surpassed anyone else's, redefining
what it meant to be crippled in a facile world.

The most extraordinary thing about her was the way
she was able to die. In the last stages of her illness she
ordered a hospital bed to be set up in the living room,
and the whole afternoon before she died, although in
tremendous pain, she received her friends and family.
Even at the end, she was making introductions,
smoothing the way, putting people at ease. "Grace is
new in town. I want you to meet her. . . Elisabeth, you
were so kind of bring me that book. . . I'm glad to see
you. . ." Already she was at the threshold of something
new. That had been true all her life.

that their home may be a haven of blessing and of peace;

Everyone has been there and felt it. There were
places in our childhood there are places for us now,
where a house is more than a house, it is a home. A
home is a state or quality of being; it exists in the midst
of a family. It is an aura, a quality of life. A home is not
something which can be bought. A home is not a piece
of real estate, although brokers everywhere would have
us believe that so much money down and so much

money per month for thirty years will equip each of us with a home. No. A home is the creation of the family formed in marriage. It goes with them wherever they go.

People ask one another, "Where is your home?" What they mean is, where were you born, or where did you live as a child, or where are you living right now? Home is the place where we may be exactly who we are, surrounded by love, where we will be accepted, whenever we arrive. Home is the place which gives us our being.

There are different kinds of homes. Not all are havens of blessing and of peace. Do adolescents always feel at home in the house of their birth and childhood? There are homes that are battlegrounds. We know them instantly the moment we enter, feel sorry for those who must live there and try to leave as soon as possible.

Some insist that even if home is not a specific house, then it is a locale, the area and atmosphere which nurtured and still brings life and spirit. "She feels at home in that part of the world."   Perhaps. But we are never at home until we are in a right relationship with others.

*   *   *

. . ."You take yourself with you wherever you go," she had said to him in a time of great inner turmoil, loss and confusion. He had heard it at other times in his life, but for him it was only a partial truth. He was himself, no matter where, only if they were together. Separation— geographic or emotional or spiritual—was unbearable, for then he was not at home. She held his heart, and in that holding, created the space in which life happened.

*   *   *

Home is the place where intimacy happens. Home
is the one place where we penetrate the deep isolation.
That is home. To be finally and truly at home is to sit
together in the late hours of the evening, and to sense
that this is the table where the saints feast in light. It is
the only place in this lifetime where we, each of us, husband and wife and children, may be finally and fully
ourselves with one another and with God. Then we are
close to heaven.

*   *   *

. . . Every member of the family had been told weeks ago
that on this June Saturday all of them would gather to
help pack up the house. It was not just any house, for it
was the house where the children had grown up. The
day had been long, hot, emotionally draining, spent
remembering and removing the furniture of a whole
life lived together.

Now the day was over. Things had been packed and
moved, placed in the garage for the moving sale, or
thrown away. What had been the place for this home
was now no longer. New homes were being formed as
the children had grown, married, moved away. Today
was the last time they would gather at the home they
once had shared.

The family had grown larger through marriage, but
everyone could still gather at the round table for the
evening meal. They were here to break bread and drink
wine to mark a memorable day and to celebrate a
birthday, the first they had shared together with the new

husband, son-in-law, brother-in-law—the most recent member of the family. Dinner drew to a close, and as he helped clear the table, he reminisced about earlier birthdays, marked by his mother's preparation of a Queen of Sheba cake, rich with chocolate, almonds and rum. Even as he spoke, the very cake, specially prepared and sent over for this meal, appeared, covered with candles. Then wine was brought out and they went around the table as each gave thanks—"for all our meals at this table." . . . "for daddy's cooking and mummy's wisdom." . . . "maybe I just can't say anything." . . . "that there are more of us." . . . "for the next time we drink wine and break bread in that new place."

When all of this was said and done, they rose from the table and went their separate ways.

through Jesus Christ our Lord, who lives and reigns with you and the Holy Spirit, one God, now and for ever. Amen.

THE BENEDICTION

It was pitch dark, but in an instant he was awake, wide awake, staring at the ceiling. The glowing red numerals on the digital clock had just flashed 3:59. As he rolled over to re-wrap his arms around her, she stirred, slightly, but did not speak. He hugged her, and whispered, "I love you."

Whenever he first awoke, no matter the hour, it was always the first thing that crossed his mind: the woman who lay next to him and how much he loved her, had loved her for a long time, would love her forever. When his thoughts got just that far, they always jolted him wide awake. For no, it would not be forever. It would be until death. How he hated that. If nothing could separate him from the love of Christ, then why should anything separate him from his love for her?

And then he knew, he always knew. So what if there were no marriages in heaven? Heaven would be far more. There was a window, a small peep hole, which gave them a glimpse of what heaven would be like; for them the window was marriage. Heaven would be marriage, blown large. For them heaven would be the kind of love they felt for one another, a love which grew, deeper and deeper—only this kind of love, the very love of Christ, will unite us all. Our life together, husband and wife, one flesh, will grow, in the twinkling of an eye, into the promise of the age to come—life everlasting.

The pain caused by even the hint of separation from her began to pass. He sighed deeply and began to pray. "O Lord, I give myself to thee this day, thine only, thine ever to be." He said it over and over and over and over and over again, until he could feel himself falling into the very abyss which the words had created around and beneath him. But he felt safe. In that abyss was God. And in that abyss was his wife, flesh of his flesh, life of his life, the very essence of love.

God the Father, God the Son, God the Holy Spirit, bless, preserve, and keep you; the Lord mercifully with his favor look upon you, and fill you with all spiritual benediction and grace; that you may faithfully live together in this life, and in the age to come have life everlasting. Amen.

REFERENCES

1. p. 23
The Alphabet of Grace
Frederick Buechner
(Seabury, New York, 1969)
p.60

2. p. 26
The Ripened Fields
Peggy Pond Church
(The Lightning Tree, Santa Fe, 1978)
Sonnet XI

3. p. 35
Church, op. cit.
Sonnet II

4. p. 46
The Corridor
Edmund Fuller
(Random House, New York, 1963)
p.41

5. p. 52
Church, op, cit.
Sonnet IX

6. p. 57
Church, op. cit
Sonnet XIV

7. p. 66
Church, op cit.
Sonnet I

8. p. 103
Anna Karenina
Leo Tolstoy
(Penguin, New York, 1954)
pp. 478-479

9. p. 105
Rough Strife
Lynne Sharon Schwartz
(New York, Harper & Row, 1980)
p. 17

10. p. 118
Fuller, op. cit.
pp. 197-198

11. p. 120
After the Fall
Arthur Miller
(Bantam, New York, 1963)

12. p. 144
Disturbances in the Field
Lynne Sharon Schwartz
(New York, Harper and Row, 1985)
p. 152

13. p. 146
Church, op. cit.
Sonnet XV

Cowley Publications is a work of the Society of St. John the Evangelist, a religious community for men in the Episcopal Church. The books we publish are a significant part of our ministry, along with the work of preaching, hospitality, and spiritual direction. We desire to provide books that will enrich your religious experience and challenge it with fresh apporaches.